through a dragonfly eye

for Bret ake David

through a
dragonfly
eye

a memoir

Seven years into my ninth decade as the
Corona virus simmers down and the climate heats up,
this is the journey of a freelance writing life.

Jenny Hobbs

19. 6. 2024

JENNY HOBBS

South Africa is a society living on a fault line and the stakes are high.
It forged me as an artist. It is who I am.
Yaël Farber, *Sunday Times*, 8 March 2015

•

I refuse to retreat into anybody's historical laager.
Solly Moeng, *Cape Times*, 22 March 2011

•

We all reinvent our pasts, but writers are in a class of their own.
Even when they know the truth, it's never enough for them.
John le Carré

•

The soul of the land is its many mothers.
Title of a painting by Nhlanhla Nhlapo

Publication © Hands-On Books 2024
Text © Jenny Hobbs 2024
First published in 2024 by Hands-On Books
www.modjajibooks.co.za

ISBN 978-1-991240-32-3 (Print)
ISBN 978-1-991240-33-0 (eBook)

Edited by Jane-Anne Hobbs
Cover artwork by Jesse Breytenbach
Dragonfly illustration by Ellie Rayner
Book design by Monique Cleghorn

Set in Sabon

Printed and bound by Creda Communications

For my daughters
Madeleine, Jane-Anne, Karen and Sophie
and grandchildren Luke, Tristan, Matthew, Zoë,
Ellie, Callum, Kate, Kirsty and Harris,
with so much love

FOREWORD

The idea for a memoir was first sparked by Professor Njabulo Ndebele's reported comment at the Dialogue on Suspect Reconciliation, a panel discussion in Cape Town in July 2010: "What South Africa needs is the entering of personal intimacies into the public space."

Njabulo and I had been co-judges for a literary prize and I value his insights. On his website, this distinguished academic and man of letters writes: "... will a new political environment emerge that will take South Africans and their country beyond 2024 with a visionary, wise, practical and decisive idealism informed by lessons from the past, a sense of urgency towards the present, while being invigorated by what the future holds?", which encapsulates the best possible outcome for our country.

The impetus to write about my life – initially for family and friends – faded in the busyness of a decade in Franschhoek. Then a few years ago, a publisher asked me to consider writing a memoir, and the journey began.

Revisiting things past has been a bumpy ride. The manuscript mutated as I shuffled through memories, discovering how much harder it is to write about yourself than create make-believe people. Since this final version is about writing as well as a blatantly nostalgic visit to the past, I have added brief inserts from my novels and short stories to suggest how lived experiences were transmuted to fiction, and some thoughts about writing.

To begin the beguine ... the title of the song Cole Porter wrote in 1935, inviting partners to join in the dance to Caribbean music:

Our forebears came from Norway, England and Scotland. The first, Donald Moodie, arrived in 1820 to join two of his brothers who had emigrated to the Cape in 1817 from their home in the Orkney Islands off the north-west coast of Scotland.

Life was hard in Europe after the Napoleonic wars. Encouraged by greedy empire-building governments, many early settlers set off in good faith to the colonies to build new lives on land they believed they had been allocated, or could purchase. By assuming the status of pioneers in untamed lands, they were involved – unwittingly at first – in the gross injustices of those times.

My story is told as a white South African against the backdrop of that history. Having led a privileged life with unusual contacts outside my community as a freelance journalist, I am all too aware of white people's wrong thinking and arrogant habits of exploitation that have resulted in three centuries of suffering endured by people of colour in South Africa under colonial and apartheid rule.

Donald Moodie joined the Royal Navy at sixteen and retired as a lieutenant eight years later. After emigrating to the Cape, he joined the colonial service and became a magistrate who spent years of his spare time in the 1820s and 1830s compiling *The Record* from official documents and oral interviews, detailing how indigenous and enslaved people were treated by colonists. It is one of our country's founding historical sources, preserved in the Western Cape Archives.

In 1930, my mother Cecilie, daughter of Norwegian immigrants, had to leave boarding school before Matric to train as a nurse because there were three younger brothers to educate. Having been denied higher education, she was determined her children would achieve it. My late husband Ron and I were the first in our families to graduate.

Six generations on, our clan are insignificant threads woven into the warp of our country's complicated tapestry, and this book is my thread. I hope it will contribute in the same positive spirit as Donald Moodie's *Record* to a broader understanding of our country's recent century, and of each other.

1

A dragonfly eye is an ingenious trumpet-shaped device about the size of your palm with a many-faceted lens at the wide end and an eye-piece at the other. Held to one eye, it fractures what you're seeing into repetitive patterns, each subtly different, which is how a dragonfly sees the world. When you twirl it, the colours in the facets swivel like a kaleidoscope.

Captivated by a dragonfly eye in a toyshop during a brief visit to Europe in 1994, I bought it, then kept it to enjoy and show visitors before giving it to my granddaughter Ellie, recently qualified in design, among a handout of special things to the grandkids. Now I've borrowed it back to survey my life from its many-faceted perspective.

Unlike details you can pin down on a page, memories are elusive and can morph with retelling. But as whole chunks of my life fade with passing years, I've been astonished by events that come into focus as sharp and bright as the day they happened, time-travelling me to places I thought I'd forgotten. And gloriously haven't.

In this mustering of a life centred on my family and enriched by reading, absorbing work, friends, and friendships with many writers, editors and publishers, you'll find a love story, two elopements, comedy, family history and ruminations about a writing career that took more than 30 years to debut between hard covers.

My earliest memory facets reflect the ward where I was taken to meet my new baby brother, after nearly three years of being the one and only. Our smiling Mum Cecilie sits up in bed near a tall arched window, holding Owen in her arms: a small blue-eyed face wrapped in a shawl.

In the next memory a year or so later, he and I are playing in a sandpit and I've taken off my broekies because the damp sand had clumped at the bottom and made them hang down. Now I'm sitting on an upturned toy bucket next to him, feeling anxious because Mum is stalking towards us pointing her camera, a Kodak with a lens that folded out of a black concertina.

On checking the photo in the family album, I see that my little peach is concealed by the skimpy dress little girls wore then. Phew.

Being born in Durban on the day of the Hindenburg disaster, 6 May 1937, wasn't exactly auspicious. The black and white news clip of the enormous airship sinking in flames shows tiny people dropping out. Their jerky figures running away from its blazing skeleton date me back to the silent movies. Incredibly, 62 of the 97 passengers and crew survived the inferno.

Also of 1937 vintage were the Golden Gate Bridge in San Francisco, the jet engine, Vanessa Redgrave, Morgan Freeman, Jack Nicholson, Jane Fonda, David Hockney, Janet Suzman and Bessie Head.

Since my birth was during King George VI and Queen Elizabeth's coronation week, I qualified as a Coronation Baby to receive an Empire porringer. It's a cumbersome china oval with a royal crest and high edges, guaranteed to cool baby porridge in seconds, and smash if it fell on the floor.

My best present was only released from its cellophane prison when I was old enough to push it along the carpet: a little gold coronation carriage pulled by horses with mounted guardsmen, all made of brightly painted lead.

Owen arrived on 25 September 1939, three weeks after World War

Two began. To accommodate his growing family, our Dad Taffy supervised a team building a house in Montclair, not far from his work managing a Merebank fertiliser factory bought by Grandpa Owen.

The property backed onto indigenous bush, and our house was an anomaly in a suburb of bungalows with red clay roof tiles made by the Marseilles company. Woodcroft was double storey and pseudo-Tudor with a wood-shingle roof, wibbly white walls, inset brick panels, and exterior 'beams' in concrete painted to look like dark wood.

Dad could never have afforded to build Woodcroft on his own. It must have been subsidised by Grandpa Owen, an English surveyor who had fled his coal-mining family for South Africa on his twentieth birthday in 1897, and become an inventor and businessman. Dad worked for him all his life, managing some of the businesses he bought. I suspect that our new home with its English airs was Grandpa's reward for a first grandson after four granddaughters.

Owen had, of course, been named after him.

In my mind's eye I can still navigate through Woodcroft, from the wide creeper-hung veranda, through the dining room with its claw-footed imbuia table, past the study with Bayeux tapestry curtains, then through the hallway to the lounge with chintz sofas, a fireplace and a mantelpiece with Royal Doulton and Basotho red clay figurines.

If the aroma of fresh bread wafted from the kitchen, it would be the first port of call to plead for a slice with melting butter and jam before heading up the stairs, past the long blue curtains on the landing, to the bedrooms.

It was up those stairs that I heard footsteps one night when I was twelve. Thinking it was Dad, I called out to him. But two jittery intruders came into my room with a torch and sat on my bed. One of them pressed a sharpened steel bar into my hand, threatening, "You shout, we kill!" As I recoiled against the wall, the other demanded the watch on my arm. I took it off with shaky fingers and he snatched it away before they sidled out towards the main bedroom.

Their torchlight woke Dad, who leapt up yelling and chased them down the stairs.

When the commotion was over, he told us that he'd jumped "clean over the kitchen table" to grab the second intruder's belt as he tried to escape after the first through the kitchen window. The leader thumped Dad with the steel bar and they both got away, leaving him with a bloody cheekbone and a black eye, swearing words I'd never heard.

My ordeal was assuaged by writing a letter about the burglary to the Junior *Sunday Tribune*, being published for the first time, and winning a guinea (riches then) for the best letter of the week. The headline read: "You Shout We Kill, Girl Told". It was triumphant compensation, and I don't remember feeling traumatised – more like one of the staunch heroines in the books I read. But the imprint of that night went deep. At times when I've lived alone, I lock my bedroom door before going to bed.

Across the road from Woodcroft in acres of neglected garden was a spooky mansion where Dad took us exploring. The panelled wooden doors to its echoing rooms had round porcelain doorknobs, and it's where I still go during house dreams: walking down a silent dusty passage lined with porcelain-knobbed doors. Only when I pored over Nigel Hughes's beautiful book *The Paintings of the Bay of Natal* in 2002 did I realise that the mansion was the homestead of the old Clairmont Estate. After the war Durban Wanderers bought it, and the renovated mansion became a clubhouse surrounded by tennis courts and sports fields.

During our later years in Montclair, the cassia hedge disgorged a rich harvest of stray tennis balls – though we first had to check underneath for puffadders that looked like dwarf stockings stuffed with birdseed. I was terrified of them, having nearly stood on one lying fatly on a sunny path when we first went to live there. Though pulled away in time by the adult behind me, its sinister diamond hatching and a fear of snakes were engraved on my mind.

We didn't have a nanny because Mum was hands-on, having enjoyed nursing babies and children during her training at Addington Hospital. She always had a cook and a domestic helper, though, who could take us for an afternoon walk if she needed to rest.

The Twenties and Thirties were hotbeds of rigorous baby-rearing theories. As we grew up, Mum told horror stories about Dr Truby King, a New Zealander whose prescribed regimen for babies was to feed them only "every four hours and never at night, and to leave them outside in the garden to toughen them up", with cuddles limited to ten minutes. Googling him now, I see he maintained that higher education for women is detrimental to their maternal functions and hence to the human race.

American psychologist Dr John Watson went one better than Truby King, warning parents against giving children too much love and affection:

Never hug and kiss them, never let them sit in your lap. If you must, kiss them once on the forehead when they say good night. Shake hands with them in the morning … Try it out. In a week's time you will find how easy it is to be perfectly objective with your child, and at the same time kind. You will be utterly ashamed of the mawkish, sentimental way you have been handling it.

It! A pox on the patriarchal thinking that still had decades to go.

The benign guru of my generation's mothers, Dr Benjamin Spock, whose sensible advice carried us through many dilemmas and crises, would have been horrified. His mantra was, "You know more than you think you do, so follow your instincts." Including plenty of cuddles.

2

My enduring memory of World War Two was being carried out to the upstairs veranda, recovering from measles and still feverish, to see the lights over the harbour.

The giant Natal fig tree by the front gate made a black pattern of branches and fleshy leaves through which the paler darkness of the sky glimmered. Slicing and stabbing like long steel knives behind the tree's familiar silhouette were searchlight beams. They moved in random jerky arcs without pattern or form in a geometric dance, until one of the beams lit on the biplane acting as a target during the practice. With chilling precision the other beams converged on the plane, seeming to hold it suspended like an insect that had blundered into a web of brilliant light. I saw the enemy hunted and trapped, and he was far more frightening than the war photos in the papers.

He was like me when I'd done something wrong and been caught.

I began to cry, and Mum held me tight saying, "Look! Look at the pretty lights!" But the image of the prisoned plane hung desolately buzzing about my dreams, and for a long time I couldn't be sure who the enemy really was. The date is in her handwriting in the foxed *Our Baby's Book* (a Pyott's Biscuits giveaway) that she filled in with her usual care: "March 1942. Measles. T 105°. Slight cough. No complications." I would soon turn five.

For sheltered southern-hemisphere children like us the war was a distant threat, though we knew that enemy submarines were prowling our coastline, and heard the rumours that German spies flashed them messages with powerful torches from beach dunes. At sunset there were no street lights, and the curtains drawn at our windows were lined with shiny blackout cotton smelling of tin trunks.

Other wartime regulations meant minor discomforts like no chocolate and cars up on blocks because of petrol rationing. White bread was a sinful luxury, surreptitiously made by sieving brown wartime flour and flushing the telltale bran down the lav. Sometimes there were weevils in the flour, and I thought the enemy may be like weevils: nasty squirmy evil creatures nibbling at our lives, a nuisance rather than a threat.

There were tangles of barbed wire on some beaches and shortages of light bulbs and razor blades. Before Dad shaved in the morning, he stropped his razor back and forth on a leather strap to sharpen the blade. Soldiers and sailors and airmen were everywhere on Durban streets, sometimes hitching lifts. Women like Mum volunteered in military hospitals or canteens, swathed in overalls.

For best in the war years, she wore a square-shouldered blue linen suit with a short skirt and her hair anchored round her head in a smooth sausage. I used to watch her roll up a strand with a hairclip-loaded pincer roller that she'd pull out carefully, leaving the hairclip in place to secure each part of the sausage. Strategic hairpins dealt with any wisps.

Grandpa Owen, whose word was law, had forbidden his sons both to go to war; they called him "The Pater" and obeyed. Colin got in first as the older brother, and volunteered to serve as a sapper with the 2nd Field Company of the SA Engineering Corps, which repaired roads and bridges and laid or defused mines. It was reckless work for a man of thirty-five with a wife and three daughters, but typical of his tackle-anything-with-a-joke approach to life.

Dad had an essential job running the fertiliser factory, though it was hard for him not to follow Colin. Like other fathers who weren't Up North fighting Germans in the desert, he rode what he called his pushbike to and from work, and every third evening pedalled to the harbour for a 12-hour Special Police Reserve shift at Maydon Wharf.

"The dry dock and floating dock were in continuous use ... I witnessed the arrival of many warships and one aircraft carrier in dire straits after battles at sea," he wrote in a notebook we found among his papers after he died.

Colin was sent to Egypt and Libya after brief training as a lieutenant. In the retreat from an attempt to relieve Tobruk, he was captured at Halfaya Pass by Rommel-led German forces in June 1942. The gunfire between the British and German tanks was so fierce that it was known as Hellfire Pass. He was one of thousands of captives who were packed into requisitioned ships and shipped off to Italian prisoner-of-war camps.

Presciently he had written to his aunt Shirley on 20 October 1941 from his tent in the Libyan desert:

My one trouble is what am I going to do when the war is finished. It will take me years, certainly many months to settle down again. I have now had 16 months of this life and feel completely unsuited for a civilian life ... My outlook on life now has so changed. I plan for today only ... [I have been] taught to destroy, people, materiel, anything and everything. Not heeding the consequences. The more I destroy the greater the deed done. Horribly warped minds we will have when we get back to a life of creating instead.

Shirley had been there for him and Taffy after their mother died early, and like her younger sister Marjorie, preferred to be called by her first name. 'Aunty' was their pet hate.

One of the few things Colin brought home after three years 'in the bag' in Italian and German prisoner-of-war camps was his army knapsack. He had embroidered it with his regimental badge, sewn in tiny stitches on the flap. Keeping imprisoned men occupied in those camps while the war raged on without them was essential to prevent depression and a sense of uselessness.

He didn't come straight home after his release and there was talk of shell-shock, though he seemed the same jolly uncle to me. From later research while writing my fourth novel, partly set during those war years, I read that the South African Defence Force used a hospital in Brighton where wounded, shell-shocked and released prisoners of war were treated. After being deloused, they were counselled by medics and psychologists before they were sent back to civilian life.

As with many ex-servicemen who suffered long-term damage after camp deprivations, Colin died of heart complications in his mid-fifties. From my novel *Kitchen Boy* (2010), at the hero John Kitching's funeral service:

In the front pew, Shirley remembers John's moth-fretted old sweaters which she'd tried to persuade him to put in the charity pile. But he'd clung to them, saying that you must never throw away warm clothing. As well as burning nightmares, he had freezing ones where his feet were in bloody rags, hobbling through snow. Nothing she could say would convince him that it wouldn't happen again.

He'd lie shivering during hot Durban nights with the curtains barely stirring at the windows, and if she touched him, she'd feel his skin as cold as a dead fish on ice. It wasn't easy living with a man whose terrors never went away. During the Vietnam war they began to call it Post-Traumatic Stress Syndrome, but she knows it as shell-shock.

After one of John's worst attacks when the children were little, his psychiatrist told her what Jean Amery of the French Resistance had written: "Those who are tortured remain tortured."

"Yes," she said, knowing it already.

"The trauma is always there," the psychiatrist had gone on. "He'll just have to become more adept at managing it. And time whittles it down."

What about her? Would she have to manage it too? For how long? But Shirley hadn't asked those questions of the doctor god.

Two TV conversations heard on the same night in 2018 shone a penetrating light on post-war trauma. Margaret MacMillan, an eminent Canadian war historian, gave the 2018 Reith Lectures on BBC Radio, commemorating the centenary of the end of the First World War. She spoke about the effects of war on veterans and civilians.

Responding to a question about the lectures from CNN's Christiane Amanpour, she said she was haunted by the words of a mother whose son took part in the My Lai Massacre in Vietnam: "I sent my son to war. He was a good boy, and they sent him back a killer."

South African artist William Kentridge's production of *The Head and the Load* at London's Tate Modern gallery, a dramatic journey about the humiliations, damage and death suffered by black African servicemen in World War One, was discussed a few hours later by three of the actors. In the Zulu tradition, Hamilton Dlamini said, "When you come back from war, you go through a ritual to cleanse yourself from the impi – 'the ugly one'."

If 19th century leaders in the southern tip of our continent had rituals to alleviate war damage, why did it take so long for 20th century army generals to acknowledge the trauma?

3

Durban was a long way from the war. We only saw the horrible photos of bombed cities in the newspapers if Mum hadn't cut them out in time. But as the last port in South Africa for troop ships going Up North and to the Far East, it was the first port when servicemen were sent home shocked and wounded, or fished out of the sea if their ships had been torpedoed in the warm shark waters of the Indian Ocean.

Durban people were proud of their reputation for hospitality. Like most families with big homes, ours took in and entertained servicemen. Sometimes Owen and I came home from school to find men in blue or khaki uniforms lounging in the low-slung veranda chairs. If they were pale and chirpy, we knew they were on their way out. Those returning or convalescent were deeply tanned against their white bandages, spoke little, often limped, and sometimes wept silent tears when they thought no one was looking. Their eyes were like our old Alsatian Leo's eyes. They sat very still and would flinch if you brushed past too close or let out a sudden shout.

Once when Mum volunteered to host two for a few nights, she was asked to take five able seamen from HMS Dorsetshire, which had been torpedoed close to Ceylon (now Sri Lanka) on 5 April 1942. They arrived in the hospital bus without caps or jackets or luggage, only ill-fitting civilian shirts and trousers. And the dazed look of men who don't know where they are.

When they arrived, Owen rushed off to tell his friends. "They've got nothing, not even a toothbrush!" I heard him yelling through the hedge, and soon his gang was standing, awed, to watch the survivors drink tea on our veranda. I stood watching too, slightly apart as befitted my status of older sister.

Though I wasn't yet five when the survivors came, I remember hearing them talk in low voices in the spare room across the landing from my bedroom, tormented by memories of their struggles in the sea. Mum's reminiscences down the years – she said I called them "revivers" – filled in the details of a short story I wrote as a tribute to her war efforts. She was thrilled to be mentioned in my friend Jenny Crwys-Williams's book *A Country at War: 1939–1945*, where it was published among factual reports about the home front in wartime South Africa.

In a letter to Jenny, Mum wrote, "They were lonely boys, so tidy; they made their beds and rolled the few clothes they had into bundles in the cupboard. Neighbours helped by giving toothbrushes, shaving gear and other necessities."

The survivors were subdued and lethargic, eating their meals in awkward silence and trooping back to the spare room afterwards to lie on their beds, smoking and staring at the ceiling. They didn't want to sit in the garden or go out to the cinema, and when our neighbour offered to take them to the beach for a swim, their refusal was vehement.

"Yer can't 'ardly blame us," I heard one say to Mum. "We was in the water for nineteen hours. Could have been et by sharks."

Seeing me in the doorway, she put on her do-this-at-once face and said, "Lovey, run and call Gertrude. I need her help with the tea things."

It was in the middle of our sticky-hot summer, and I'd be lying awake under a cotton sheet. That was the summer I learnt to eavesdrop as a way of finding out the things grownups wouldn't tell me. They never seemed to realise how far their voices travelled at night.

4

Probably to prove that he could be as brave as his brother Colin, Dad swam out during the war to a shipwreck off South Beach to 'liberate' a wire cable sheathed in black rubber, then wrapped it round his body to swim back to shore, nearly drowning under its weight.

He used the cable to make us a giant stride – a single-strand swing hanging from the extended branch of a tall tree, with a pipe triangle at the bottom. You held onto the lower edge of the triangle while running in a wider and wider circle until you were whizzing round through the air, taking exhilarating leaps when your feet hit the ground.

Other shifts of the wartime patterns in my dragonfly eye were the Sunderlands (transport planes that could land on water, known as flying boats) taking off and landing like birds of burden near Maydon Wharf on Durban Bay ... laughter over a poster that read 'Keep Mum About Ships' ... adults confiding fears they thought we couldn't hear.

Everyone wore hats on the street. My favourite photo of Dad, dashingly suited with a tilted felt hat, was taken by a street photographer who'd snap pedestrians as they approached, then give them numbered tickets to buy prints.

Then there was the thrill of my first piece of Chiclets chewing gum, donated by a friend whose father had fought with the Yanks in Italy. A precious piece of chewing gum would last for weeks if joggled with sugar in a Lion matchbox tucked into my broekie elastic at the hip. There was endless talk of the Blitz, Churchill, the Battle of Britain, Hitler, Nazis, absent fathers and buzz bombs.

Going on six, I had my first intimation of the mysteries of sex. Owen's gang of four-year-olds wanted to know what girls looked like. He said if I took my broekies off and lay on my back on the nesting boxes in the abandoned duck house facing the entrance with my legs apart, he'd let them in one by one for a look, charging a penny a time which we'd share.

It sounded like a good proposition, so I agreed.

The duck house was in the neglected vegetable garden, with low concrete block walls roofed by half a corrugated-iron rain tank painted green. The dry duck poop on the earth floor crunched under bare feet.

One sunny afternoon while Mum was resting, I shed my cotton broekies, lay down as instructed under the roof ticking with heat, and opened my legs for the boys to look at my nethers.

They were not complimentary.

"Is that all?"

"My mom's has fur on."

"I can't see anything. Pull your skirt up higher ... I *still* can't see. It's too dark. Want my money back."

"You already came in," my brother snapped.

The first two voyeurs discovered that dry duck poop exploded if stamped on, so the gang crowded in to join them, creating a fine rising miasma.

"Can I touch your thing?" one persisted.

"No!" Their hands were like coalminers' coming off shift.

"Please? It looks nice."

My first compliment from a boy but I said louder, "No!"

The heat and whiffy haze stirred up by stamping boy feet weren't part of the deal. I grabbed my broekies, wriggled off the nesting boxes, slunk past flailing arms and legs, and escaped to the consoling shade of the mango tree. And the later realisation that I'd been conned. Owen said they'd demanded their money back because my thing wasn't worth it. They'd been cheated.

Girls had *nothing down there.*

At five and a half I had gone eagerly off to Convent High School near Albert Park, which taught all ages from Class 1 to Matric and was accessible by a single bus ride.

The Holy Family nuns were strict. After the alphabet, they drummed in our times tables – still automatic 80 years later. Sums and letters had to be written neatly in pencil, progressing to joined-up writing between parallel lines. We were taught to hem white cotton squares and knit with needles squeaking on hot days – tedious tasks obliterated by hours of reading at home. Being called a bookworm was a badge of honour then.

The Convent uniform was tussah dresses with red buttons, white panama hats and red-striped black blazers. Tussah was rough natural silk from India, less expensive than cotton from distant countries across seas patrolled by hostile submarines.

At morning assemblies we lined up along the slanted-brick edges of curving tarmac paths as Mother Superior presided from a low balcony. There was endless speculation about whether she and the gliding nuns had hair under their starched heart-shaped wimples or had shaved it off?

In Standard One our desks had inkwells for dipping pen nibs that scratched across pages where writing would smudge if not blotted – or worse, disgorge a blot and give you inky fingers. These quibbles apart, I was happy learning new things and journeying to and from school on my own in the bus.

A lingering memory of the Convent is being smacked hard on the thigh by a senior nun for sneaking up forbidden steps to the higher classes to see an alleged burglar's handprint on the wall.

"I'll leave my handprint on *you*," she said, and did. It was bright pink and lasted the whole day.

5

In Montclair there were no girls of my age living nearby, so books were my friends – either lying on my bed reading or climbing a tree with a book.

Crucially, our parents were readers and Dad was a storyteller. Mum took us on regular visits to the Durban Junior Library to appease my book habit. She also subscribed to *The Children's Newspaper,* which came in the post from England for a few years after the war, turning me into a lifelong news junkie.

The distant war backgrounded our lives for nearly seven years.

In the gung-ho spirit of the time, we drew Spitfire silhouettes with RAF insignia on their wings in our jotter margins. Life was simple for primary school kids then, with competition limited to Sports Day, spelling tests and end-of-term class results.

Owen was lucky to have friends of his age living nearby. When they didn't come to play with him, we'd take turns whizzing round on the giant stride, or trundling down the quiet side road on his box cart with pram wheels, or pea-shooting with hard black canna seeds through short lengths of thin bamboo. We scooted bumpily along crazy-paved paths, played with our Slinkies and Pick-Up Sticks, rolled dice for Ludo and Snakes & Ladders, and built contraptions with his Tinkertoy and Meccano.

After he was given a pair of white mice, I helped him create an intricate cardboard village padded with cotton wool in Grandpa Owen's old tin trunk. They always seemed to be canoodling and soon grew to a smelly horde, which Mum eventually banished to a pet shop.

The next craze was silkworms fed with small branches of mulberry leaves in shoeboxes with punctured lids. Watching them spin cocoons on the branches was fascinating, followed by winding filaments of silk onto cardboard batons as the released cocoons bobbed in water – only a few before tedium set in and we lost interest. Then the shoeboxes with their burden of dead leaves, worm poops and shrivelling cocoons were gone too.

To Mum's dismay I spurned dolls except for the first, Rosebud, who had a cloth body, real hair and life-like limbs. I cut her tummy open to see what was inside, but she spilt sawdust and I had to borrow a needle and thread to sew her closed again. A swan-necked white plaster bust we called (obviously) Neck was much more fun than a doll. She came with three wigs for her bald head, and wipe-off makeup, with greasy black eyebrow pencils we used for drawing moustaches when we dressed up.

In retrospect, Rosebud, I take back every dismissive comment and apologise for my clumsy surgical stitching. Under your wooden face and real hair you couldn't eat or talk or wet or walk, but you never lost your dimpled smile. Recently I've seen you resurrected on an episode of the *Antiques Roadshow*.

If the weather after school was fine and not too windy I'd climb a tree, though it had to have visible branches: the Natal fig by the gate was too big and entwined, harbouring insects, if not snakes. Once when I'd climbed up into a high fir tree at our cousins' Hilton farm – easy but scratchy, and bendy at the top – Mum stood below shouting at me to come down and I declined.

Such moments of defiance were rare. After transgressions, she'd mastered the "Now you've disappointed me" face. Or she'd call me "a wild woman from Borneo". That must have been common mum-speak then, because my contemporaries remember it too – alternating with, "You look as though you've been dragged through a bush backwards."

The best climb was up the smooth-barked flamboyant tree on the edge of the front lawn with a book, Marie biscuits and some diluted Oros, to wedge into a V of branches, reading and dreaming.

If the ice cream man came trundling along the road on the tricycle with a big white box in front, ringing his cozening bell, I'd scramble down calling for Owen and we'd run inside for an advance on pocket money. When the box's lid was opened, wisps of mist wreathed the dry ice where ice creams nestled like glittering jewels. Eskimo Pies and Twistees were the best, though a little pot of vanilla ice cream with a wooden spoon lasted longer and didn't drip.

I don't remember winter in Durban. Just hot, very hot, or windy.

6

The bus to and from school ran along Clairwood's main street and through Umbilo towards Albert Park and the Embankment overlooking the harbour.

Clairwood was still shuttered on the morning journey, but on the way home the street effervesced with busyness. Keening music and wafts of curry and frying samoosas drifted out of higgledy-piggledy shops, spilling their goods on the pavements: racks of dazzling saris, gauze scarves, rolls of oilcloth, jumbled pairs of sandals, pyramids of aluminium pots, folded-open hessian bags heaped with red and ochre spices, bunches of herbs and drying leaves.

On festival days, the bus inched past exuberant processions with garlanded gods on platforms wheeled by devotees and chanting followers, whiffs of incense and marigolds, and hectic drumming. If Dad drove us through Clairwood at night during Diwali, the lovely Hindu festival of lights, there'd be rows of little clay-bowl oil lamps flickering along walls and windowsills, an enchanting transformation of everyday life.

Memories of these daily journeys to and from school through Clairwood gave me the background for my second novel. As readers do, I made lists of words I liked the sound of, or wanted to remember, and collected the fancy names scrolled on the backs of Indian buses. One of them was *The Sweet-Smelling Jasmine*, which decades later featured in my second novel and became its title.

Twice a day the *Jasmine*'s worn tyres would squeal to a halt at the bus stop next to the pharmacy and stand shuddering and backfiring with Ram Pillay revving the engine vigorously so it wouldn't give up the struggle and expire before it reached the station terminus. It was often so full that its windows bristled with the heads of passengers gasping for air. Roped to the roof rack there'd be shabby suitcases and rolled mattresses and sacks of mealie meal and rice, surrounded by produce on the way to and from the market: crates of windblown fowls crouching in terror, lettuces and pumpkins and pineapples, bunches of litchis and heavy trusses of green bananas. Boys would be clasping the brass pole in the doorway like clusters of ticks. At each stop they'd let go and scamper off to make room for the descending passengers: old people feeling for the steps, large women landing with a double thump of sandals, sticky-faced children tumbling down. After them came a waft of stale air that had been used and re-used since the last stop ...

Everyone hurried because Ram Pillay's foot sometimes slipped off the clutch, making the *Jasmine* lurch forward, taking unwary limbs with it. When he had relocated the clutch and finished apologising and begun revving again, the bus would let out a belch of exhaust fumes before bounding forward in convulsive jerks as the boys grabbed for the brass pole, competing to see whose feet would be snatched up last from the dust.

An exception to Clairwood's bustle was the pharmacy, a brick-built temple of hygiene raised above its humbler neighbours by opposing concrete stairs with display windows of toiletries at the top.

Inside was an aura of hallowed medication with a background of mysteriously labelled wooden drawers in cubby-holes – "Latin," Mum whispered – and shelves of home remedies like Grand-Pa Headache Powders, Syrup of Figs, Dettol and Eno's Fruit Salts. The chemist wore a starched white coat multi-buttoned up one side to the neck. To concoct a prescription, he'd withdraw to an inner sanctum to mix or decant it, then proffer it in a pillbox or a brown ribbed bottle with a hand-written label bordered in blue.

Glass counters displayed more toiletries in the pull-out drawers below: April Violets talcum powder, 4711 Eau de Cologne, and special soaps like Pears and Vinolia. Controversial goods – enema bulbs and sanitary pads – were stowed out of sight and had to be requested. All purchases were wrapped in a neat green paper package secured with sticky-tape. Discretion was absolute.

Mum's training as a nursing sister emphasised a vitamin-packed diet, so we had fresh orange juice first thing in the morning. Every week the neighbourhood vegetable vendor padded up our drive with double-cupped wicker baskets hanging from both ends of a pole across his shoulder, heaped with fresh fruit and vegetables.

Greeting everyone with his palms together and smiling under a shaggy white moustache, he'd lower the baskets and squat to offer fragrant speckled mangoes, branches laden with plump litchis, cupped hands of ladyfinger bananas, pawpaws, granadillas, and shiny-fresh purple brinjals and other vegetables that didn't interest us then.

Lettuces had to be washed in a solution of permanganate of potash in case – you never know – they'd been grown in nightsoil. For a former nursing sister, hygiene is forever paramount.

In this second passage from *The Sweet-Smelling Jasmine*, the Clairwood we left when I was twelve had coalesced with my adolescence into a fictional teenage character, Isabel, newly arrived at an imaginary South Coast village called Two Rivers. She is fascinated by the contrast between her home in a conservative Transvaal mining town and the still-mixed community on the Natal coast in the early Fifties.

The mango tree leaning over the wall served as a private place to read and an observation post for watching people. Zulu women from the reserves come to town for supplies, their hips padded for extra fullness under voluminous skirts, their hair built up with red mud into stately Nefertiti coiffures. Demure Moslem women in narrow pastel tunics and trousers, heads wrapped in silk scarves with the ends floating behind as they walked. Bargain-hunting housewives from the company estate in Horrockses cotton frocks and shady slumming hats, picking their fastidious ways between wads of chewed sugarcane. Hindu women with oiled hair in heavy buns and tiny jewelled studs winking in their noses ...

I'd been transported from a quiet house with aging, ailing parents into a noisy subtropical marketplace where people walked and talked and argued with each other, brushing shoulders and mixing together as though the laws we lived under, and I had thought immutable, didn't exist. It was like shaking a kaleidoscope, then finding when you put it to your eye again that the chips of glass had changed places and fallen into a startling new pattern.

Re-reading this piece written in the early 1990s reminds me how persistent the image of a childhood toy can be – to the point of buying the dragonfly eye, drawn to it by the memory of our cardboard kaleidoscope.

7

Besides adventuring into the spooky house across the road, Dad took us walking in the bush, scrambling over monkey vines and bird watching, while Mum took us on city treats. *Bambi* and *Fantasia* were my first movies, and I was entranced by the University of Cape Town ballet company's performances of *The Nutcracker* and *Swan Lake* with its four tripping little cygnets in bouncy white tutus. Dancing was too sissy for boys then.

Once she took us to the Metro to see the organist Tommy MacLennan rise out of the stage on 'the mighty Wurlitzer' in a paean of bone-thrilling music, bathed in floodlights and baring a Kolynos toothpaste smile above his tuxedo. After such splendour, the film that followed was an anticlimax.

Another treat was gliding up the long escalator to the second-floor tea-room in Payne Brothers on Smith Street, to claim our reward for an ordeal at the dentist, whose slow drill resonated in your head like a buzz saw. The escalator had a panoramic view of the ground floor, from Gents to Haberdashery.

Our reward was a Knickerbocker Glory, queen of the milk bar. It came in a tall flared glass so you could see the layers of fruit salad alternating with scoops of vanilla ice cream and sticky red syrup, topped off with a swirl of whipped cream, dribbles of chocolate sauce and hundreds and thousands crowned by a glacé cherry. Owen didn't like glacé cherries, so I ate his too.

He was a believer in mysteries and I the know-it-all older sister.

For years I teased him about his claim one Christmas morning to have spotted the edge of Father Christmas's robe *whisking* out the door from the upstairs veranda, netted against mosquitoes, where we slept in summer.

He was too young to come to Sunday school during my brief holy period walking down to the church at the bottom of Blamey Road with Shirley, an older girl from next door, dressed in our best frocks. My class sat in a ring of chairs under a flame tree, picking its brown velvet flower buds and biting off the pointed tips to squirt their nectar at each other.

Once we trooped into the graveyard to see if there were any bloodstains after hearing that a young girl had been strangled on one of the graves. Which grave was the question. Our search didn't turn up a single bloodstain.

Familiar tastes and smells are potent revivers of memory. Chocolate-tasting Maltabella porridge for breakfast ... maas set on a warm night under a layer of sourish cream ... the caramel aroma of boiling sugar-cane juice wafting up from Hulett's sugar mill down by the river ... the fragrance of frangipani and yesterday-today-and-tomorrow bushes in the garden ... tasselled green mealies being stripped for boiling ... freshly woven reed mats like a grassy welcome.

The smell and taste of guavas are a less welcome memory, as they go back to my perch in the palomino branches of the guava tree. You sometimes had to spit out incautious bites of yellow guavas if half-worms wriggled out of the place you'd just bitten into. Even worse, after seeing the stinky sewage tanker's segmented trunk slurping out the septic tank, I was told that its overflow went into a French drain that nourished the roots of the guava tree.

Only years later did I realise that the pungent whiffs of what I'd always thought was gardeners' tobacco had been culled from dagga plants flourishing in unvisited corners of gardens where they worked, the leaves dried and rolled into *zols* using pages from discarded telephone directories.

8

Every July during the war and a few years after, Mum took us by train to visit our Norwegian grandparents in Zululand for a few weeks of pampering. We didn't realise that she needed pampering at that stressful time more than we did.

Our holidays began on the evening train that went north to Gingindlovu, Mtubatuba and Gollel. Drawn by a chuffing steam engine, it negotiated the points out of Durban station and crossed the Umgeni bridge before picking up speed. We clickety-clacked into the night, past houses and dark patches of bush, lamplit clusters of huts and once a moonlit Hindu temple in a grove of mango trees and bamboo.

Train travel has the world streaming past as poles flick by carrying rows of dipping and rising lines. Leaning out the window of a steam train risks getting smuts in your eyes, so we watched through the glass until it grew dark, the cabin lights flicked on and the louvred shutters were pulled down.

The top bunks in compartments were folded up during the day and the leather seats had a fat round matching leather bolster at each end. Windows were etched with a Springbok head, and blinds and shutters could be pulled up and down independently. A hinged wooden table between the windows folded inwards before you hooked it up to display a stainless-steel washbasin with press-down taps for face-washing and tooth-cleaning. Drinking water had to be tapped from tall glass cylinders at the ends of the corridors, where it sloshed back and forth with the train's movements, getting unpleasantly warmer.

Soon the bedding man came with big canvas rolls to make up our beds: crisp cotton sheets under dark blue blankets with SAR&H embroidered in red. We hauled ourselves up to the top bunks using green leather handholds slung like long thin sausages under the carriage roof, hanging our outer clothes on the door hooks to snuggle down in vests and broekies. All night our clothes swayed against the door as the train galloped on, thundering over bridges and through tunnels, leaning sideways through curves. Every now and then it would slow down to slide into a station where slivers of light and passing voices came through the shutters. Sometimes there'd be a wheel-tapper chink-chinking along the train with his hammer before the whistle blew, the train jerked forwards and we were on our way again.

Sleep came rocked in a cradle of creaking wood and leather with a smell of cinders in the darkness. You'd wake in the night to realise the train had stopped in the still darkness, then drowse off when it began to move again.

In the morning we tumbled out of our bunks with the first grey light and tugged down the shutters. There at last under a sunrise sky were the Zululand hills, rocky outcrops, domed grass huts, twiggy thorn trees, orange-tipped aloes, occasional farmhouses with clusters of sheds.

Later we'd navigate the shifting corridors to the dining car for breakfast: bacon and eggs and sausages, or bubble 'n squeak, the ultimate leftover: a fried concoction of last night's potatoes and cabbage with chopped-up bacon. Back in the compartment, the excitement mounted. From Mposa to KwaMbonambi where Mum had grown up, then at last Eteza station where our grandparents would be waiting, their breath puffing in the cold air as they waved and smiled.

"Yennifair", they called me as they enveloped us in hugs.

Bestefar and Bestemor could have come from a traditional primer: they were affectionate, welcoming, generous, wrinkly and *old*.

Bestemor, Stena Böe, arrived in Durban from Bergen in 1898 to join her brother Petro, a photographer, and remembered curtseying in the street to the composer Edvard Grieg before training as a children's nurse. Her father was a pastor who ministered from a ship sailing up and down the Norwegian coast as far as Lapland. In Durban she worked for the Egeland family; one of her charges was Leif Egeland, who later became the South African High Commissioner in London.

Many descendants of Norwegian communities in Kwa-Zulu Natal contributed their skills to our country: Larsens, Rosholts, Grinakers, Lunds and more. Nils Eckhof was a plastic surgeon at Guys Hospital during the war where he helped reconstruct damaged servicemen's faces.

The Norwegian national dress, Hardanger brooch and beaded red cap sent to me after the war as the eldest granddaughter have been worn by my daughters and granddaughters.

Bestefar, Bernt Jacobsen, came from a family of captains and shipbuilders in Arendal at the southern tip of Norway. Part of his Hanseatic League heritage was the *labskaus* Bestemor made, a hearty sailors' dish of tinned bully beef, potatoes, onions and beetroot.

Bestefar arrived in Durban in 1902 on the sailing ship *Erik Dahl*, captained by his uncle. He first worked on a farm to improve his English, then for ships' chandlers as a bookkeeper. After he met and married Stena, they had two children before moving to Empangeni where he managed a store and saved until they could afford to buy a small sugar farm at KwaMbonambi in 1917, with two more children in tow.

9

Fifteen years later, the sugar farm failed during a serious drought and the Depression. As motivated immigrants do, they borrowed enough to buy the trading store at Umfolozi village and the old country hotel next door.

Bestefar had bags under his eyes and a big schnozz like a naartjie – the legendary 'Jacobsen nose' inherited by many of his descendants. In Umfolozi he created a network of small businesses that he ran from an office at the back of the house.

Bestemor was a classic apple-cheeked grandmother in loose crêpe de chine dresses who spoilt us with floppy heart-shaped waffles from a round waffle iron on her coal stove, and Q-shaped *Berlinerkranser* biscuits. My fond illusion that the Black Magic chocolate box in her wardrobe filled itself overnight evaporated when I saw her replenishing it one day.

Bestefar drove us home from Eteza station in his big black Buick, going hell for leather over the corrugations on the gravel road. Umfolozi village was a handful of whitewashed buildings with green corrugated iron roofs: an old house which had once been a country hotel, trading store, storerooms and a butchery. Over the way were railway sheds and a doll-house station at the end of a branch railway line that served the nearby sugarcane farms.

Further down the sand road, Bestefar had established a sawmill on a low hill overlooking the cane lands of the Umfolozi Flats and Lake Eteza, a shallow reed-edged stretch of water with crocodiles floating half-submerged or sunning themselves on the mud banks.

The old house at Umfolozi was wreathed in a vast golden shower climber and shaded at the back by the usual huge Natal fig tree. In the danger spectrum of my earliest Umfolozi memory is a cobra rising above baby brother Owen asleep in his Moses basket under that tree. I called out in terror and the snake subsided as we were snatched away. No doubt Freud would have made a meal out of my snake fears.

Each of the house's tall fly-screened windows had a little tin roof above it to keep out the sun. In the living room was a black leather chaise where Bestefar took forty winks after lunch under a blanket of many-coloured crochet squares. On the mantelpiece, a wooden clock chimed the quarter hours ('ding-dang-dung-dong') and a wireless crackled out the news three times a day.

The bedrooms opened off a long corridor with coir matting: high ceilings with massive wardrobes and beds with white cotton counter-panes and folded paisley eiderdowns. On each marble washstand would be a white china water jug and basin. At night we'd wash our faces in the basin before cleaning our teeth, then spitting into the enamel slop bucket below. Spitting into a slop bucket is more fun than into a basin; you aim for the covered hole in the middle of the lid and score points for direct hits or the quickest-sliding gob.

We slept under mosquito nets that Mum tucked in under the bed-clothes after she'd kissed us goodnight. It felt good to lie in the dark knowing you were safe from the mozzies whining against the net-ting in a frenzy for your blood. During the day, the nets were knotted up out of the way to hang like giant white chrysalises from their ceiling hooks.

At the end of the corridor was a bathroom with an enormous claw-footed enamel bath, stained under the taps. The tap water was unpredictable because the borehole tank on stilts had long green algae beards inside. Sometimes there'd be frantic tadpoles or tiny frogs swimming in the bath, sources of delicious terror in case they wriggled up the wrong place.

The diesel engine pumping the water also ran the lights. It throbbed outside in the pump house all evening like a heart beating, unnoticed until it switched off. Then the light bulbs died to an orange glow and went out, and a black silence spread through the house. After that you had to use candles or torches. Candlelight and the smell of warm wax always remind me of Umfolozi, as does the scent of naartjies. The orchard where fat orange fruit hung among glossy leaves was the first place we ran to on our first morning, to gorge ourselves until juice ran down our chins and stuck our fingers together.

From there we'd run across the yard to the store and through the screen door to the busy back section where our friend Percy Jackson was in charge, wearing a safari suit, his hair slicked back with Brylcreem above a big shy smile and a thin moustache like Clark Gable's. He played the accordion and a guitar and kept crocodile eggs in a sandbox on the sunny steps at the door. They'd hatch into tiny snapping reptiles that scared shrieking customers before being returned to the lake. Percy became a crocodile expert, and years later we saw him in the *Farmer's Weekly* featured as The Crocodile King of Zululand.

The store's wooden floor was worn and gritty from all the feet shuffling in and out, and gave off dust overlaid by the smell of new clothes and paraffin. Shelves up the walls held patent medicines in red and yellow boxes, packets of seeds and blue-wrapped candles, stacks of black-edged enamel plates, billycans, coiled belts with round brass buckles, shoeboxes, piles of felt hats, bales of dark blue and brown German print (now called shweshwe), grey blankets, bottles of boiled sweets and brown paper packets of beans, rice and gov'ment sugar.

From the ceiling hung swaying racks of shirts, dresses, headwraps, overalls, gumboots, black umbrellas and bicycle tyres. We'd sit on the wooden stepladders behind the counter, watching Percy and his assistants reach up for them with long hooked poles. Sometimes there'd be a squeak of pulleys as a rack was lowered for a customer to choose from. If people didn't move away smartly, they'd get lost in forests of clothing or banged on the head by gumboots.

Often, each item was paid for as it was pushed over the counter, and only when change had been given would the next thing be asked for. "Penny stickies," a customer would say. One box of matches on the counter, sixpence paid, fivepence change. Then, "tickey sugar" or "shilling paraffin" or "mealie meal, one bag" and the same exchange took place with no complicated adding.

Percy gave us motto sweets in fancy pastel shapes with words on them: 'Ek het jou lief' in faint red letters, or 'Baby come duza' or 'Kiss me sweetheart'. We liked those hard scented sweets because they lasted. Bestefar was usually working in his office in the house, but if he came into the store while we were there, he'd give us each a bee-hive: a silver-wrapped chocolate blob with sweet creamy white foam inside, topped by the ubiquitous glacé cherry.

Through a door behind the counter was the storeroom with piles of cardboard cartons and heaps of hay-smelling jute sacks perfect for climbing on. If you poked your fingers into a sack, you could feel what was inside: stamp mealies, mealie meal, peanuts or dry beans. We made forbidden holes in hidden places for the pleasure of feeling streams of grain slipping through our fingers.

Percy kept a mongoose in there to deal with rats and snakes; if teased it darted forward and tried to bite us.

Then there was the excitement of the daily train, and when we were older, playing on the stationary goods trucks it brought.

Every weekday at noon there'd be a toot-toot among the thorn trees along the branch line from Eteza and a steam locomotive came chuffing in backwards, pushing a guard's van and empty trucks. The brass pipes would be shining, the engine driver grinning above his elbow hanging out the window.

Half the village turned out when the train came, to help unload or just stand and watch. The truck doors clanged open. Boxes and cartons and sacks and farming implements were hustled out. Canvas post bags were dumped on the platform from the guard's van. Drums rumbled down gangplanks. People shouted. Dogs barked. In the open trucks on the other siding, the last bundles of sugarcane were stamped down into place. A ganger uncoupled the emptied trucks, signalled the driver to shunt forward with the guard's van, then back into the other siding to have the loaded ones hitched on. At last the station master's whistle blew and his green flag dropped. There was a jerk and the clamour of couplings as pistons began to move up and down, the wheels turned and the train chuffed away through the thorn trees back to the main line.

Into the trading store went the sacks of mealie meal, stamp mealies, peanuts, rice and gov'ment sugar carried on bent backs; cartons of cigarettes, sweets, groceries and bales of blankets and cotton goods piled on wheelbarrows; barrels of diesoline, oil, paraffin and petrol rolled hand-over-hand in the dust.

The petrol was for the tall red Pegasus pump in front of the store with a metal jacket padlocked over its two glass cylinders. To fill a petrol tank, the attendant unlocked and opened it, then pushed a long handle back and forth, pumping golden liquid up into one of the cylinders until it was level with the gallon mark, then let it run down a thick ringed hose into the tank or jerry can. There weren't many cars in those war years, just the odd Ford and dusty farm lorries. Bestefar's Buick was sometimes down in Durban helping the war effort.

Men loaded bundles of sugarcane all day during the winter season, their shoulders padded with sacks as they ran stooping up wooden gangplanks to heave in the bundles. On quiet afternoons we'd climb up and down the iron ladders of empty trucks on the lake side where we couldn't be seen from the house, sometimes asking for a stick of sugarcane ("*Cela uMoba* please?"). Sugarcane has thick maroon skin that you'd shave off with a penknife before biting off chunks to chew and suck. The gravel round the station was littered with peels and spat-out sugarcane fibre.

At other times we'd head for the sawdust mountain behind the sawmill, along the sand road with its grass *middelmannetjie* oily from the sumps of logging lorries, bowling hard green monkey oranges down the wheel ruts.

You heard the sawmill before you got there: logs whining against saws in an open corrugated-iron shed where everything was coated in spraying sawdust – machines, trolleys, overalls, even the eyelashes of the men using the saws and heaving pine and gum logs around. The warm resiny smell in there was different from the nose-tickle of drying wood in the timber yard, where planks were stacked criss-cross with air spaces between them. Walking between the high stacks was like being dwarfed by skyscrapers.

The sawdust mountain was a moonscape of hills and valleys, grey on the surface but moistly yellow inside. When we dug into it to make caves, the damp sawdust clung to our hands and legs and feet. "Don't go in deep, you hear? Or it'll collapse and bury you" was the stern warning from the foreman.

If we'd agreed on a time with our friends the Roberts kids, who lived on a farm across the lake, we'd wave flags at each other: torn pieces of sheet fixed to long bamboo poles. Once when I'd spent the night there, Mrs Roberts told Mum that she'd found Sally and me leaping up and down on our beds shouting "Jumping bosoms! Jumping bosoms!" Still flatter than pancakes.

Beyond the Roberts farm was the rail-cum-road bridge to Mtuba-tuba where drivers had to stop their cars and listen for trains before scooting across on loose-laid railway sleepers that rattled. We loved the spine-tingling danger of crossing the 'clank-clank bridge' as much as the thrill of being taken to the circus on a starry night with gum trees flicking past the car windows.

My most powerful Zululand memory is this: I feel the winter cold on my cheeks as Mum and I walk along the gravel road one evening with thorn trees silhouetted against a vermilion sunset. I ask, "Why is the sky so red tonight?" and she answers, "They say it's because of dust in the atmosphere from the atom bombs dropped on Japan."

We had stayed longer than usual. It was early August 1945.

10

My journey as a writer began with a love of stories: being read to every night, older people talking about their lives and the world when they were young, and – above all – the engrossing world of books. Maurice Maeterlinck's book-of-a-play *The Blue Bird* and its beautiful illustrations saw me through a tonsillectomy at six. Dad's wondrous copy of *The Ship That Sailed to Mars* by William Timlin, given to him by his stepmother for his birthday in 1930, was a particular favourite.

Another was *Tales of a Russian Grandmother* where people drank their tea from glasses through sugar lumps, and families slept on the stove. I couldn't imagine how a family could fit on the Defy, until I learnt that during the harsh Russian winters, people slept on tiled platforms heated underneath by wood fires, called stoves.

The weirdest books were the German *Struwwelpeter* with rhyming cautionary tales and *Fattipuffs and Thinifers*, translated from a French children's book by André Maurois, where Fattipuffs lay on their beds surrounded by food with sweet drinks on tap, while Thinifers were starving, stick-thin and gawky. Besides its threatening tone and unfunny cartoonish illustrations, Thinifer was far too close to my full name Jennifer.

Most afternoons I'd be reading about amazing adventures: following honeyguides through the bush in *The Long Grass Whispers* (a book of African folk tales about animals, translated by Geraldine Elliot), sailing in junks, riding horses or clunking wagons across the prairies, or singing my way around the world as a wandering minstrel. Bestemor had a record of a soulful man singing "A wand'ring minstrel am I, a thing of rags and patches", which she'd play on her wind-up gramophone.

In 1946 I fell for a bomber pilot, Wing Commander Guy Gibson VC, leader of RAF 617 Squadron (the Dambusters), whose autobiography *Enemy Coast Ahead* was published posthumously in 1946 with his handsome smiling photo on the cover. He'd been killed on a mission in his Lancaster bomber towards the end of the war, and I grieved over his book whenever I picked it up.

Being transported to other times and countries is one of the great joys of reading. Rudyard Kipling's *The Jungle Book* and *Kim* took me to India, Mary Grant Bruce's Billabong series to Australia, Johanna Spyri's *Heidi* to Switzerland, Mark Twain's *Huckleberry Finn* to Mississippi, John Buchan's *The Thirty-Nine Steps* to Scotland.

Durban Junior Library books marched along the shelves soberly clad in caramel-brown leather. The few illustrations were pen and ink. My treks through boarding school and ballet series led to Arthur Ransome's *Swallows and Amazons*, and I begged for some copies of my own. At Mum's suggestion, Bestefar and Bestemor arranged with Griggs bookshop for me to go in and choose one every month for a year until I had all twelve – a prolonged Christmas gift of reading about English children having enviable adventures.

With few exceptions, the books we read came from England.

The late, great Chris van Wyk told a story for our times in *Ouma Ruby's Secret*, about his grandmother who took him as a boy into second-hand bookshops in Joburg where she'd buy a book he chose, then ask him to read it to her when they got home. He only realised when he was older that she was illiterate, not having had access to education during apartheid, like so many of our elders. Chris became a writer, poet and storyteller who could mesmerise a hall packed with school kids, and keep audiences of adults riveted by tales of his childhood in the sand-blown lee of mine dumps, always with heart

43

and humour. His going too early was a grievous loss to our writing community.

But his children's books live on for today's youngsters, who should have access in libraries and school libraries to the abundant variety of mother-tongue books with dazzling illustrations by local authors and illustrators. Gcina Mhlophe and Niki Daly were in the vanguard of storytellers writing books for our children.

The shameful fact is that government funding for reading, the essential skill for education, has been pitiful. The 2021 Progress in International Reading Literacy Study (PIRLS) to test the reading comprehension of children in their fourth year of primary school, when they are supposed to graduate from their mother tongue to English, found that 81% of South Africa's learners can't read for meaning in their home language.

It's only thanks to extraordinary efforts by dedicated reading initiatives like READ, Biblionef, Book Dash, the Children's Book Network, Fundza, Nal'ibali, Pukupedia, Rally to Read, Wordworks and privately funded school libraries in townships and rural areas that books are belatedly reaching more youngsters.

My greatest privilege has been constant access to books and the fulfilment of daily reading.

11

World War Two ended when I was eight and left powerful memories, reinforced by decades of watching war movies and reading books about the war – even today, as writers resurrect family histories and discover hidden stories. Now my grandchildren study the world war I lived through in their history lessons or lectures, my life having spanned hand-cranked telephones to hand-held cellphones as powerful as computers, and bulky cars with running boards and dickey seats to sleek electric sedans.

VE Day in May 1945 had erupted in a celebration of flags and church bells and cheering that the war was over, though Japan only conceded later, after the atom bombs devastated Hiroshima and Nagasaki.

In 1947 I was one of the excited Convent schoolchildren waving little Union Jacks in Durban's West Street as the British royal family drove by, waving graciously. Mum and her friends doted on photos of the Queen Mother and the princesses in their frocks and hats, though there were indignant mutterings in communities further north about the way Jan Smuts lavished attention on the royals. That show of colonial pomp and ceremony surely contributed to his and the United Party's surprise defeat in the 1948 election.

No one predicted the gruelling decades of apartheid that would follow.

In the Forties and early Fifties I grew up in our family's white enclave. We kids were taught to greet and be polite to all elders, especially those who worked for our family, and never to leave our things lying around for someone else to pick up. But like most white people then we took the unnatural gulf between us as a fact of life.

Homework and after-hour activities in junior school were minimal. When we got home, we'd kick off our shoes and socks and spend the rest of the afternoon climbing trees, riding bikes, lying on the grass looking up at the changing clouds, or burrowed into a book or comic.

Owen bought Superman and Batman comics with his pocket money, and as the superior older sister, I bought Classic Comics. Of course I read all of his too and soon we'd accumulated a knee-high pile. One day they were gone, leaving only the Classic Comics. He had swapped all the others with his gang for marbles. I was furious and we came to blows, during which he moaned loudly – as was his habit when I asserted my rights – "Jennifer's *hurting* me!"

Guess who got the sympathy.

What we wore then didn't matter as much as cleaning our teeth and washing behind our ears. Our mothers worried about us standing on a snake or crossing busy roads or climbing too high and falling.

The little mirrored cupboard above the bathroom basin held Mum's remedies for ailments: Syrup of Figs for constipation, Phillips Milk of Magnesia for runny tummies, mercurochrome for scratches and grazes, eucalyptus oil rubbed on our chests for colds, Friar's Balsam in a bowl of warm water with towels over our heads to inhale the steam up blocked noses. For fevers we were given M&B – May & Baker sulphonamide tablets crushed in a spoon with jam.

Though she was fussy about us wearing hats in the sun, there was no effective sun protection then. All we had was cool pink calamine lotion to soothe sunburn and chickenpox, but peeling off sunburnt skin in patches was fun. Mum never embarrassed us with the gentian violet dabbed on the poor railway kids' ringworm – though 20 years

46

later, I was dabbing our kids' ringworm with a transparent sheep remedy prescribed by a veterinarian friend.

Mum's weapon against worms was a fat pink knitting needle, brandished every six months, which she used to probe the contents of the loaded potty we had to produce. When she took out the pink knitting needle, we'd brace for worm muti. In my time, if you saw your kids scratching their backsides, the advice was to pull down their pyjama bottoms while they were sleeping and shine a torch on their anuses, which was supposed to make pinworms emerge and wave about.

I didn't stoop to that indignity for mine, but with dogs in our home, we dispensed six-monthly doses of worm muti to them all.

More shifts of the dragonfly facet patterns as the Forties moved on:

Fishing for grunter in the harbour with Dad and Owen in a small boat with an outboard motor, during which I learnt to thread live earthworms onto hooks without flinching ... pulling the boat up the beach at Salisbury Island for a picnic ... Fifi, our low-slung black Citroën with two upside-down Vs on the radiator and a slender bonnet with prominent headlights on the fenders (Rowan Atkinson drives one as Maigret in the TV series) ... sharing a slab of chocolate with Dad if he fetched me from school, usually scoffing it all before we got home, united in guilt.

Chocolate was a devourer of pocket money too. Sometimes I'd buy a quarter pound of chocolate-coated raisins or peanuts – "goats" we called them, for obvious reasons – at the tea-room where I got off the bus, and finish them engrossed in a book.

12

At ten I was moved to a new school, considered old enough to change from the Montclair bus near Durban Tech to one of the sedate trams trundling up Berea Road and along Musgrave Road past Durban Girls College.

Mum had boarded at College from Zululand before having to leave early because there were younger brothers to educate. She must have felt the old sting of her disappointment at not being able to write Matric as she watched me walk down to the bus stop in the mornings after we had checked my satchel with her mantra: "Season ticket – hanky – lunch".

Do men still carry hankies? Then, a father asked to wipe a child's cake-smeared mouth might pull out of his trouser pocket a checked square of fine cotton knotted with dried snot, or used to clean his fingers after wrestling with an oily wheel nut.

At College there were lay teachers and no wimples, other prayers at assembly, hockey instead of netball. We wore dark green uniforms: dresses in summer and scratchy gyms with broad pleats girdled at the waist, square-necked white shirts and dark green blazers in winter. Same white panama hats with dark green trimming and a different badge. Hair had to be kept under close arrest in plaits or constrained by black bands called snoods. For a while, Mum patiently wove two thick plaits in my long hair, curly and reddish brown then. I still have a hank from when it was cut short at twelve, though now my hair is what I choose to call platinum.

At this and my next school, there were tweedy British-trained single women among the teachers, many having lost fiancés or husbands during the world wars. These teachers' scholarly code, salted with sardonic humour, demanded work and application. As in most schools, only a few were truly inspiring.

Running down the corridors was *not done*, I discovered after cantering round a corner and colliding with Miss Middleton, the formidable College headmistress, who grasped me by the shoulders and jumped me aside with a stern warning to *behave*.

During my entrance interview with her and Mum, I'd ventured that I wanted to travel one day to the places I read about in books, so it was agreed that I'd learn French rather than Latin. Though I took a year of French and another of Special German at university, neither included conversation.

When I later complained of being language-deprived and asked why Mum hadn't spoken to us in Norwegian and Dad hadn't encouraged us to speak isiZulu with the staff in our home, they had excuses – chiefly that when we were born, people believed that more than one language would confuse children.

They were wrong, and should have known from personal experience that kids soak up languages like sponges. Your home language is a useful and effortless skill to pass on to the next generation – and parents with different home languages give double value.

Unfortunately my sole language is English, with basic Afrikaans learnt at school and improved in Franschhoek, plus smatterings of French and German and memories of lilting Norwegian. To partly atone for this deficiency, I try to greet people now in their home languages, especially isiXhosa which prevails in Cape Town.

An enduring memory from College is a girl called Evelyn telling a horrified group of us with our heads bent towards her that a man's 'thing' was as long as her forearm. The only 'thing' I knew was Owen's little willy in the bath. After Evelyn's revelation I'd glance sideways at men in the streets wearing the baggy trousers of the times, wondering where and how they hid their enormous appendages.

Dad didn't seem to have one, though when he grew older his balls drooped out of his fishing shorts if he sat manspreading on a hot day.

Other shifts of dragonfly patterns from the College years include singing the school hymn *He Who Would Valiant Be* and carols at Christmas, especially *The Holly and the Ivy* with its lovely refrain:

> The rising of the sun
> And the running of the deer
> The playing of the merry organ
> Sweet singing in the choir.

Singing together has been one of the joys of my life. The first hit song I remember was from 1949: *I'm Looking Over a Four-Leaf Clover.*

Miss Middleton was complemented by an equally formidable elocution teacher, Miss Sneddon. She taught us to enunciate, emphasising the consonants, this never-forgotten verse:

> To sit in solemn silence in a dull dark dock
> In a pestilential prison with a life-long lock
> Awaiting the sensation of a short sharp shock
> From a cheap and chippy chopper on a big black block.

It must be a standard exercise for drama students because the actor playing Prince Charles blurts it in the Netflix series *The Crown.*

Elizabeth Sneddon became an icon of the South African theatre world when she was appointed Professor of Speech and Drama at the University of Natal in Durban, and galvanised generations of actors and playwrights.

News that the Nationalists had won the 1948 election broke at an Umbilo bus stop on my way home from College, and caused an uproar in the bus. This unexpected setback was followed by weeks of baffled fury that General Smuts had been defeated – and unseated! – after helping Britain to win the war, as we'd been told. Repercussions echoed round staunchly United Party Natal with shock-horror newspaper reports and outraged grumbling over late-afternoon spots of gin & tonic about Nat gerrymandering.

There was no concept of the seismic changes to come in our country. Post-war schmaltz was *in* and the promises of peace were coming true ...

Until January 1949, when there were riots in Durban as Zulu mobs attacked Indian shop owners after an incident with a fleeing shoplifter. Stores and homes were looted and set on fire and 142 people died. As we're still learning from recent rioting, xenophobia flares to sudden violence when isolated shop owners are unable to defend themselves from crowds of enraged, often unemployed, looters taking revenge for their poverty and hopelessness.

The grim tentacles of migrant labour, broken families and the aftermath of decades of apartheid ethnic cleansing continue to strangle our country.

We kids were hustled off with Mum to Shirley down the coast at Umzumbe, while Dad held the fort at Fison's fertiliser factory on Maydon Wharf, where he had been appointed manager when Grandpa Owen sold the Merebank factory. The workers called Dad *intshebe mbomvu* (red beard) because of his still-ginger five o'clock shadow in the afternoons.

Walking through Fison's giant warehouse among soaring pyramids of fertiliser was a mythical vision of symmetrical tumuli bathed in slanting beams of daylight from its high clerestory windows. The other-worldly scent of one heap was so intriguing that I asked Dad for a matchbox to put some in to take home, though when opened, the scent had evaporated.

Above all, there was the rich aroma of rain on Durban's dry earth after a hot day – petrichor, such an intriguing word.

13

Highlights of the Forties and early Fifties were snazzy milk bars with swivelling stools and jukeboxes. Today's impersonal ice cream counters aren't a patch on them – or the serene Creamery in Maritzburg with its black-and-white tiled floor and rainbow array of flavoured syrups for milkshakes.

Nearby was Ogilvy's shoe shop with its instant X-ray machine where you put your feet into a cavity wearing different pairs of shoes, to see in a green panel how well your toe bones fitted. Needless to say, it was soon banished as dangerous – especially for radiation-overdosed shop assistants.

In the late Forties the New Look was all the rage, though fuller skirts took time to reach South Africa. Nobody could have dreamt that in less than 50 years, the roomy jeans we wore to picnics would get fashionably tighter and darker, then artfully torn in places.

At the cinema we followed the bouncing ball above words on the screen to sing along, watched drummers introducing the weekly African Mirror newsreel before a cartoon (*Tom and Jerry* or *Loopy De Loop*), then a travelogue with a sonorous voice-over ending "... and as the sun sinks slowly in the west ..." During the interval, usherettes in maroon uniforms with gold epaulettes sauntered down the aisles with trays slung from their necks, selling Eskimo Pies, tubs of vanilla ice cream, *Stage & Cinema* magazines and cigarettes.

Audiences stood up after smoke-wreathed movies for *God Save the King* and later *Queen*, except for the unpatriotic few who slunk or stomped out. All the seat-arms had ashtrays. TV only arrived in

South Africa in 1976 because President Verwoerd believed that its effect was akin to poison gas. Albert Hertzog, Minister for Posts and Telegraphs, opined that "... the effect of wrong pictures on children, the less developed and other races can be destructive".

School-learnt poems have long lives. Once in an airport shop I found a nifty book called *I Wandered Lonely as a Cloud ... And Other Poems You Half-Remember From School*, which evoke fond reminiscences, as do radio jingles.

> Singin' in the bathtub, singin' for joy
> Livin' the life of Lifebuoy
> Can't help singin' cause I know
> Lifebuoy really stops B-E-E-O. [Sung on a descending scale.]

Or the most memorable of that era:

> Brylcreem – a little dab'll do ya
> Brylcreem – you'll feel so debonair
> Brylcreem – the gals'll all pursue ya
> They'll love to run their fingers through your hair.

As if!

Ballet classes at Eileen Keegan's school were held in an old building opposite the West Street cemetery. Random fiddling with its brass light switches gave shocks. An elderly lady with bird's nest hair sat at an upright piano in the corner tinkling out music for our exercises; years later I realised that the familiar music had been Chopin.

Ballet classes were more hard work than dancing. During the seven years when I jetéed and pliéed and laboured at the barre trying to 'tuck my bottom in' (impossible, as it goes out), we only had one concert in the City Hall. I was a clown and took part in a Spanish dance with a long skirt and a hibiscus flower behind my ear, but that was the sum total of my stage career.

On the floor below Eileen Keegan's, there were tap-dancing classes that looked like fun, though ballet was The Thing for middle-class girls then. Tap was what immigrant girls with pierced and ringed ears did. But if Shirley Temple and that debonair smoothie Fred Astaire could tap dance, why not Cecchetti non-achievers like me?

How fashions change, along with pretensions.

14

It's tempting to assess how your parents measured up after you've been through the parenting process yourself.

Whatever we remember of ours, my brothers and I were privileged children who grew up in the loving security of a home with parents who did their best for us – to the point where they stayed together for more than 50 years, despite their differences and a few shaky years during the war.

Our Dad, Taffy, added an invaluable dimension to my life. Because of him, I learnt not to fear or distrust men, to love books and reading, to enjoy puns and laugh at rude jokes, and to fossick in second-hand shops and sale rooms.

He was Natal born and bred, living on farms as a child and speaking fluent isiZulu all his life. A slender, active boy with bright red curls and the freckled, sun-sensitive skin that went with them, he grew into a stocky man with a boep and calves like the old Coca-Cola bottles. He started to go bald early and asked us kids to rub his scalp in the mornings to encourage his hair to grow again, but it just got thinner and greyer.

Dad worked diligently all his life managing Grandpa Owen's businesses. He was generous, gregarious, single-minded, pig-headed, and prone to losing his temper in spectacular but brief outbursts.

Fishing was his passion, and he was also a fine craftsman. I remember sitting on a windowsill with my sandals on his workshop bench, watching him plane a piece of wood with aromatic shavings curling over his stubby fingers and freckled forearms. He would beaver away in the workshop, a cigarette hanging from his mouth, surrounded by humming machines and sawdust, and flanked by an old wooden wireless half as tall as me, turned up loud. On the dial were stations like Hilversum and Schenectady.

He continued to make well-designed furniture until he couldn't work the lathe any more: tables, stools, revolving bookshelves and canvas-seated roorkhi chairs, as well as a rocking horse, a doll's house, a wheelback high-chair, plywood jigsaw puzzles, wooden toys and blocks for the grandchildren when they came along.

In the war years Dad would quote snatches of school-learnt poetry while stropping his razor in the morning. Favourites were Milton's *Lycidas* – "Yet once more, O ye laurels, and once more / Ye myrtles brown, with ivy never sere" – and the witches' speech in *Macbeth*: "'Aroint thee, witch!' the rump-fed ronyon cries." He loved the witches' speech with its menacing: "I'll do, I'll do, and I'll do."

He was not a literary man, though read a lot: Kipling, O. Henry, Alexander Woollcott, Churchill, Lawrence Green and Martha Gellhorn, an intrepid war correspondent and Ernest Hemingway's third wife. Dad would have been tickled to know that I met her during her visit to South Africa the year before she died at eighty-eight. She signed his copy of her book *Travels with Myself and Another* for me. He had been gone for a decade by then, but it gave me great pleasure. *Another* was, of course, Hemingway, unused to being out of the limelight.

Dad had an eye for bargains in the auction rooms and junk shops where he rummaged, bringing home slightly damaged treasures he could fix, like old brass scales redolent of justice, as if it is a measurable ideal rather than a human endeavour that too often fails. He taught us to appreciate second-hand furniture with good lines and dovetail joints, and to look for signs of woodborer. Besides chocolate, he also brought unusual treats home. A week before one Guy Fawkes night, he was in the dogbox after breezing in with a firework the size of a Mazawattee tea tin, costing all of a pound and a half. Owen and I fawned over it with his gang while Mum moaned about the expense. Yet when lit, its display of popping fireballs and sparkling fountains went on and on, to be remembered all these years later – the ultimate in value for money.

Dad's roving interests made him a sucker for new gimmicks which he'd fall for and buy, like a big-bellied glass ostrich that went on dipping its beak into a glass of water ("Perpetual motion, see?"), then wonder what to do with. There was a day when he came home beaming with a tiny transistor radio broadcasting from his shirt pocket.

One of his virtues was his biggest fault: he told spellbinding stories, but as he grew older, they were told over and over again. While strangers hung on his tales of elephant-bone collectors in Maputaland (the bones to be used for bone-meal fertiliser) and the prodigious size and number of fish he had caught, the family's eyes would glaze over. We had heard it all before. When he nailed people at parties with long-winded anecdotes, we winced. But when our children came along, he enchanted them with the stories we had heard too often.

At a different time, with his storytelling facility and observations of river life, he could have written a book like *Tarka the Otter*.

He was affectionate and more soft-hearted with me than my brothers. The only time he ever smacked me, he tucked me into bed afterwards with tears in his eyes. When my brothers grew up and challenged him, he'd blurt at them in a temper, then forget what he'd said and be hurt when they stayed angry. He thought fathers should be obeyed as he and Colin had obeyed The Pater.

He was very close to Colin; they called each other "Prick". Grandpa Owen took them camping in the bush as boys and taught them to fish and shoot guinea fowl and buck. Dad cast his first fly for trout in 1912 when he was five and must have known every trout water in Natal by the time he died in 1986 at seventy-nine, a doyen of the sport. He'd have been pleased as Punch to know that his great-grandson Tom is a Junior Springbok fly-fisherman.

When we were older, he taught us to shoot with a pellet gun, aiming at empty tin cans upside down on fencing droppers, which would spin around if hit. Years later, manfully hiding his white knuckles, he taught me to drive. "Just remember one thing about driving," he said as he tottered off for a stiff whisky after the first lesson. "Everyone else on the road is a bloody fool."

One of his ambitions had been to own a Rolls-Royce. In the late Sixties he bought a run-down 1935 convertible and spent years restoring it with loving care, ordering spare parts from England and shaping by hand the wooden pieces that needed replacing. Its numberplate was, fittingly, NP 2222. Too-too too-too, the epitome of elegant motoring.

He became a menace on the road, driving it with cavalier disregard for other drivers, seldom looking in the dim rear-view or side mirrors, hogging the right lane and making wide hand-signalled turns that sent lesser cars scattering. After we had all left home and the parents downsized to a garden flat, he sold it for a song, having had his enjoyment from the fixing.

Only when his cough became persistent was he persuaded to give up smoking, considering himself far too healthy to succumb to others' ailments. After a session in hospital for what he called a brontosaurus to check an ominous shadow on one lung, it turned out to be harmless – as he had predicted, asking what all the fuss was about. His greatest fear was to have what he called "mice in the basement" – prostate cancer.

When that was diagnosed a few months later, Mum withheld the diagnosis as the doctor had said his heart would probably give up before it became a problem.

Dad knew the stretch of Umzumbe coastline intimately, having holidayed there since he was ten. At low tide he'd poke around with a gaff for redbait under ledges he kept secret, or drag out a squirming octopus, cut off a leg for bait and put it back again to grow a new leg. He lived with nature, not off it.

One midwinter day, fishing alone on a farm dam near Nottingham Road, the anchor of his small boat stuck in water weeds, and he climbed overboard into icy chest-high water to cut it free. He drove home freezing cold and wet, and had a heart attack that night, followed later by a stroke.

For nine months he struggled to get well again. An active, self-willed man all his life, he railed against having to stay in bed at the mercy of women – Mum with her nursing experience and careful roster of helpers, and the kind strong Zulu woman who lifted and turned him.

For nine months he was convinced he would get better. He made notes in writing that grew smaller and smaller, a shadow of the elegant flowing script he had been so proud of. The last time I drove down to see him in the bedroom crammed with his most precious belongings – family photos, books, an old brass barometer, bundled trout rods, flat square tins of trout flies, his silver cup for winning the under-16 hurdles at school, his tweed deerstalker cap with earflaps, the wood samples on his desk next to the dented hip flask he carried when fishing, all the paraphernalia of a vigorous life – he mumbled, "I'm dying, aren't I?" and I had to answer, "Yes."

But I had time to thank him for being such a good father to me. He slipped away a few weeks later, followed by a funeral service packed with his extended family, friends – mostly trout fishermen – and former employees, one of whom gave a eulogy in isiZulu.

Rest in peace *intshebe mbomvu* [red beard], son of KwaZulu Natal.

My brothers and I inherited two invaluable genetic gifts from him – energy and optimism. He wasn't ambitious beyond the imperative to catch bigger trout than fellow fishermen, and content with his working life as long as he had time for fishing, crafting wood, and a few laughs with friends over a whisky.

15

By contrast, Mum felt unfulfilled as she grew older. Like so many women of her generation, she had given up her career for marriage and children. As we daughters gained new freedoms, they felt trapped in the role of 'the little woman' to traditional husbands with power as the breadwinners who signed the cheques.

Wives needed their permission to open a bank account until a few decades ago.

Cecilie had been a bright, stylish nursing sister at Addington, planning to apply for midwifery training in England when she met Dad. He shared a yacht on Durban harbour with friends, and they fell in love during a whirl of sailing and picnics. As an immigrants' daughter, she had to brace herself to visit his imposing father and stepmother Nita and their gracious rambling home overlooking Maritzburg.

But her courage prevailed. They were married in 1934 on her parents' small drought-stricken farm at KwaMbonambi. In the photos of the wedding party, the Walters men wear top hats and the women long Thirties dresses and garden party hats. Bestemor and Bestefar are in their Sunday best. The smile on Mum's face is confident, though Dad looks politely apprehensive. Lacking a mother from an early age and a sister, schooled at boys' schools and shyer than his ebullient older brother, he probably didn't know much about women.

They honeymooned at the Polana Hotel in Lourenço Marques, we two children arrived after a while, and life in the new Montclair house was all she could have wished for. During the turmoil of World War Two, however, their marriage was shaken by meeting more like-minded others. The possibility of divorce was concealed from us.

Grandpa Owen supported Mum through the ordeal, furious with his younger son, whom he banished for a year to do solo penance in a remote hut by the lagoon at Sandwich Harbour in what was then South-West Africa. His task was to manage a team loading and trucking bags of accumulated bird guano from the lagoon island along the beach at low tide to Windhoek, where the bags were railed to the fertiliser factory. The abundant fishing on the deserted coastline must have mitigated his loneliness.

In 1947 he was back with stories of diamond smugglers sneaking past in the night, a rusting ship's bow sticking out of a sand dune, sheets of pink flamingos on the lagoon, and a restless ghost that opened and closed the doors of the hut until he'd cleaned up the graves behind it.

Our life went on as pleasantly as before. In time we became a two-car family, with a boxy Willys station wagon parked next to Fifi. Before he died in 1986 Mum and Dad celebrated their golden wedding anniversary.

A few years later, Mum confided that he'd wanted to leave her during the war because he'd met someone more compatible while away on fertiliser business. She didn't mention that she'd kept letters from an Irish doctor warmly thanking her for wartime food parcels sent to his mother, which we found among her papers after she died. As a former nursing sister, she venerated doctors.

Family secrets have a way of slipping out when least expected.

In 1950 she had surprised the socks off everyone by producing a baby brother at thirty-nine, which was *old*. Owen and I knew the facts of life by then and couldn't believe she and Dad were still Doing It.

In those days women had frog tests to find out if they were pregnant. A researcher had discovered in the 1930s that the female platanna (African clawed frog, *Xenopus laevis*) would produce eggs within 12 hours of being injected under the skin with a pregnant woman's urine. My generation of young women were still schlepping our pee to doctors for these tests in the early Sixties. The good news was that the injected frogs didn't die and lived on – sometimes for more than ten years – to be used again. The bad news is that the frog test was so effective that platannas were exported to laboratories all over the world carrying a fungus with them that has wiped out countless populations of frogs.

Since the survival of frogs is one of the eco-markers of the climate crisis, this is very bad news indeed.

David was born with jaundice and looked like a calm little Buddha sitting in his pram.

From Mum we children inherited her keen intelligence, her determination, and her Norwegian sense of orderliness. She was prone to attacks of Ménière's disease that made her dizzy and meant lying in the bedroom with the curtains closed for several days. Most of her energy was spent on creating a well-run home for us and making sure we had the advantages she'd been denied. She strove to play by the rules of the times and her profession, which meant vitamin-packed meals and essential injections.

There was one alarming hiccup. During the polio epidemic in the early Fifties, we weren't allowed to do anything strenuous like ride bikes, and had to rest in the afternoons. So it was a shock when Owen developed polio just before writing Matric. He was isolated in the fever hospital, where it was diagnosed as bulbar polio, which could lead to total paralysis in an iron lung. However, blood tests showed that he'd been exposed to the virus several times before and had antibodies. When the fever went down, only a muscle in his upper lip was paralysed, with a sole after-effect: he could no longer whistle.

Our parents knuckled down to more than 50 years of marriage and a quiet life ambling along with different interests. Mum gardened, took a keen interest in politics, wrote poetry and fiery letters to the newspapers. We lived too far away for me to be an attentive daughter beyond regular phone calls and occasional visits, so we weren't close as she aged, dealing bravely with macular degeneration in the retirement village where she moved after Dad died.

Having quizzed her doctors about the reason for her fading vision when it was diagnosed, she warned me years ago that my blue Nordic eyes, like hers, were at risk in our fierce sunlight. I should always wear shady hats or caps in the sun and polarised sunglasses, and take zinc and selenium tablets. Since then I've used the specially formulated pills now available (Ocuvite) and have mercifully retained my sight.

Mum had high aspirations for all three of us and it was a given that we would go to university. In return, as mothers do, she took well-earned pleasure in our achievements.

Owen followed his namesake grandfather by studying land survey and working all over Natal and on the triangulation of Botswana, bringing home hilarious stories. His extended performance of dung beetles zooming in on fresh poop in the desert had family and friends crying with laughter for years. After several farming ventures, his wife Gilly's idea to make and sell nougat expanded to a successful business, Wedgewood (now managed by one of their sons), which also sells and exports scrumptious biscuits.

All Owen's friends called him Taffy. It must be catching.

David studied Fine Art with Michelle and they married after graduating. He became one of our country's best-known ceramicists, working with Michelle's close support from a series of old buildings that could accommodate a pottery and living space. Dad in his seventies helped him to rebuild the derelict water mill at Caversham in Kwa-Zulu Natal to create a studio, toiling side by side to replace the wooden blades on its huge millwheel. Sadly it was washed away with the wood-and-iron mill when the Lions River flooded in 1986, though their stone-built home and gallery survived.

David's friends also called him Taffy. It's definitely catching.

Grown older now, I feel more and more sorry for Mum and her generation of wives whose ambitions were set aside as they concentrated their energies on helping their children claim the liberties they couldn't have.

I only realised how indomitable she was when we went to say goodbye to her in the funeral parlour. In death her face was not that of the failing, nearly blind 84-year-old Mum I had last seen, but of a resolute Viking queen facing death with her Jacobsen nose held high, like a longboat prow.

16

My dragonfly eye moves away from parents to focus on our treasured family holiday place in Umzumbe.

An hour's drive south of Durban, the N2 highway crosses the uMzumbe River meandering through its silted-up estuary. Upstream, hills recede into a blue distance stippled with huts and patches of bananas, amadumbes and mealies. Cane fields and areas of natural bush make it a tranquil and lovely scene in the slanting sunshine of late afternoon, though haunted by rural poverty unknown to the holidaymakers under a scattering of umbrellas on the beaches.

Umzumbe has a history that includes raids by Shaka's impis and an influx of missionaries with their condescending assumptions and resolution 'to save heathen souls'. The damage inflicted by the rigid religious beliefs of white missionaries on indigenous cultures is widely acknowledged and deplored. On the positive side, however, they established clinics, schools and colleges. Many of South Africa's older leaders and writers were educated at mission-funded establishments, with promising students awarded bursaries to further their education overseas.

Shaka's half-brother Mpande, who became king in 1840 after overthrowing Dingane, was open to the growing number of missionaries in Natal and to isiZulu translations of the Bible.

We have a graphic roneoed account of the first missionaries' arrival in Umzumbe. None of them were related to my family, but their stories epitomise the later Victorian era in Umzumbe.

Shortly before the outbreak of the American Civil War in 1861, the American Board of Commissioners for Foreign Missions sent the Rev Elijah Robbins and the Rev Henry Bridgman out to their Zulu Mission in Natal, to be followed later by their wives. Amy Bridgman, Henry's daughter, wrote in a 1935 memoir:

After riding a hundred miles on horseback, they suddenly found themselves on the rim of a huge bowl. Before them a wild tumble of green hills. Zulu kraals crowned many of the hill tops and herds of sleek cattle and goats grazed peacefully over the luxuriant green spaces. Winding in and out was a silvery stream, the Umzumbe River, and the deep ravines on either side were lined with bush.

Whipping up their horses, the two Missionaries rode down, down into the centre of the bowl. Here they found a tiny hill and riding to its crest, they dismounted and took possession of that hill – and that green hill so far away became the centre of the future Umzumbe and its Mission Station ... They bargained for bundles of thatch grass in exchange for mirrors, knives and other trinkets, and built a protective wigwam round the trunk of a big tree before retreating inside.

Very soon the shadows began to lengthen: the sun went down. The crowd of natives disappeared and darkness enfolded the earth. Immediately the African night sounds began – far in the distance hyenas could be heard barking and howling. Nearer and nearer they came, a whole pack of them, until, at last, the hideous creatures threw themselves upon the thatch lean-to where the reverends were sitting with their backs against the tree trunk, holding their guns loaded and cocked. The bedlam of unearthly snaps and snarls, howls and growls kept up the whole night through, except when the wolves stopped to sniff and smell just the other side of the thatch.

When their wives joined them in Umzumbe in 1869, their wattle-

and-daub houses were a sore trial, with thatched roofs and floors of pounded earth smoothed with cow dung and ashes. Mrs Bridgman's treasured horsehair-padded furniture suffered from dust sifting down from the thatch. Open windows let in swarms of insects and framed the faces of curious visitors. She asked American friends to send cheap muslin, then sewed the strips together to make a ceiling of sorts and screens for the windows.

Amy went on:

I remember so well hearing my Mother tell of her first experiences at Umzumbe. She said that when she first saw the people in all their nakedness, she wanted to cover her eyes with her hands, and didn't see at all how she could live in that place for ever and ever.

As Amy's mother Laura had feared, missionary life was an ordeal, but they soldiered on: Laura in a crinoline with a black lace fascinator over her head. She was an ardent temperance worker, and in her spare moments classified and painted watercolours of wildflowers, a collection now in Boston.

She had her lighter moments too. Amy wrote of her mother's annual trek to preside at the Women's Christian Temperance Union:

Her trip to Maritzburg once a year became almost an emancipation for her, a chance to escape from the bush life for a little while and to mingle with those of like tastes for just a few days. And how Mother did prink and brush up for that great occasion!

Gradually the Missionaries made friends with eight or ten Chiefs and from them, one by one, they got permission to start a school or mud-walled Church on their tribal land.

The reputation of their kindness spread far and wide. People with sores, aching teeth and other afflictions came to them for help. It was a marvel to have a tooth pulled quickly. Holding the head of a sufferer firmly between his knees and using forceps, Henry Bridgman had the troublesome tooth out in a fraction of time ... A chicken a tooth was the price of relief, so always the yard was filled with cadaverous fowls.

Along with tooth-pulling, Mr Bridgman gave advice about sick cattle and gardens. Mrs Bridgman advised mothers about their babies. Young girls fleeing from an unwanted marriage also came for asylum until things could be straightened out with their irate fathers and prospective grooms. As numbers grew, a girls' boarding school developed and opened in 1873 ... later absorbed into Inanda Seminary.

Three generations of the Bridgmans served in South Africa, the younger ones as medical missionaries or teachers. In 1916 they took charge at Umzumbe, where "they started a night school for herd boys in Umzumbe, and often as many as 20 attended. The boys slept in a large hut and left silently at dawn to attend their herds".

The Umzumbe district seems to have been catnip to missionaries as godly pioneers continued to arrive. Fairview Mission Station was founded by the Rev Noyce of the American Methodists; he bought the 2,400-acre farm Fairview where he opened schools. In 1930 he persuaded his Board to sell 1,500 acres to 'Native tenants', a move bitterly opposed by local farmers, though the mission avoided land-ownership laws by retaining possession and granting rights of occupation. By 1965 most of Fairview had been allocated, and today many Zulu families have been settled there for decades.

One of the lots belonged to our friend and former housekeeper, the late Irene Ngcobo, and is now occupied by her son Michael.

Dominican nuns established St Elmo's Convent in 1918: a group of Italianate red-brick buildings that once housed a boarding school for learning-disabled youngsters. When funds ran out the school was closed, leaving St Elmo's brooding forlornly over the village, fallen into disrepair, occupied by squatters.

Perhaps there is a special need for holy help on this part of the coastline? When an elegant holiday home with upward-swooping Thai gables was built on Lady Moor Place, villagers called it 'The house of horns'.

More seriously, the missionaries' successes are reflected by the 84% of South Africans who identify as Christian, however intermingled with traditional beliefs.

17

Since my first visit to great-aunt Shirley's home Craigievar as a little girl, I've spent a lifetime of holidays in Umzumbe. It has always been a place of the heart for our family and many cousins, focus of happy memories.

Natal Government Railways started running a South Coast railway line from Durban in the 1890s to bring supplies and holidaymakers to the villages and beautiful beaches, returning with loads of sugarcane. Umzumbe village grew around a station next to a seaside farm bought in 1916 by Dad's grandmother, Charlotte Moor, blessing five generations of her descendants with beach holidays.

Like the N2 highway, progress has largely passed Umzumbe by. For years it has been a haven for fishermen, retired people and families who holiday in the cottages or the congenial Pumula Beach Hotel overlooking the sea. Our red-brick cottage was built by Dad in 1962.

It's peaceful and private and surrounded by dense dune forest: umdoni, milkwood and ficus trees, rustling clumps of wild bananas, glossy-leaved amathungulus and mop-headed dracaenas. The birds in the bush range from Natal robins that carol us awake in the morning, to tinker barbets, purple-crested louries and the rarely seen narina trogon. Wave rhythms send us to sleep at night.

A much-climbed red milkwood sprawls along the edge of the bank, invaded when the fruit is ripe by a troop of monkeys heralded by soft foot-thumps on the roof. This is the signal to close doors and windows to prevent marauding for fruit. We've also seen them tease the *mpiti* [blue duiker] that graze in the cooler hours in the glade below, their little tails flicking.

In the glade are trundling shongololos, skeins of cobwebs glinting with dew in the morning, and in the evening, bats swinging down for insects and fireflies. On the far side of the glade, a sand path runs between low dunes laced with creepers to the beach, with sentinel aloes.

The bush-fringed Umzumbe bay has long scallops of clean sand between ridges of basalt and quartz rock, with swimming gullies and intriguing rock pools for kids. The main beach opposite the hotel is known to surfers for its right point break. Schools of dolphin curve down the waves as they patrol the bay, and between May and September, humpback whales cruise beyond the wave-line to and from their breeding grounds off Mozambique, sometimes with calves as their numbers increase.

If there has been no rain to bring down the river in a muddy flood tossing with uprooted debris, the sea varies from celadon to mossy greens, and is seldom too cold for swimming, though it can be dangerous at high tide, with unexpected rips and currents. We teach children to watch the sea before swimming, to stay within their depth and keep touching the sand with their feet, to beware of the undertow (Garp's 'Under Toad') and never to swim alone.

But even adults aren't as careful as they should be. After decades of swimming in a familiar gully, I was one of three who could have drowned on the wild stormy day in 1991 when the cruise liner *Oceanos* sank 100 kilometres to the south. Though we'd watched the sea before going in, we were overwhelmed by a freak wave that swept us towards a ridge of rocks and a fierce outward rip. Coming up gasping between two strong men saved me and we made it back to the beach, chastened and shivering.

Everyone aboard the *Oceanos* was rescued by South African Air Force helicopter pilots.

Across the river mouth towards Splash Rock, you can walk for a solitary hour, watching seagulls and scavenging crabs tittuping sideways on the wet sand with their granadilla-pip eyes out on stalks. A gale is an exhilaration of scudding clouds and spray flying off waves, leaving the beach fringed along the wave line with glassy chunks of jellyfish and stranded bluebottles.

Dunes are part of the magic of Umzumbe, an endless diversion for kids to climb up and jump or slide down. Once after a storm exposed a midden of calcified mussel shells and sharpened stone scrapers on a high dune at the point, we imagined early *strandlopers* surviving on mussels.

When there is no wind, we'll sit on the home dune with glasses of wine at sunset, watching the sea and sky darken to deep blue and swifts looping over the bush for insects. In the bay below, hunting turtles may come up for air in the waning light: dark oval shapes in the water with archaic heads on skinny necks.

To find yourself, as I did once, surfacing face to face with a quizzical green turtle is a mystical experience tempered by the thought: what if they bite?

18

Darwin is said to have written, "It is not the strongest of the species that survives nor the most intelligent, but the one most responsive to change." We are all survivors of resilient forebears who endured centuries of hardship. Especially mothers whose stamina and courage have carried them through multiple childbirths, often in gruelling circumstances, to nurture the children who lived.

Our great-grandmother Charlotte Moor features in my late cousin Robert Moor's privately published family history, *Journey to Avalon*. After he retired as a Cambridge don, Robert researched original scripts, personal reminiscences and the extensive library facilities available to him in Cambridge to write this comprehensive and incisive book, from which I quote below.

Charlotte and her siblings had a tyrannical magistrate father, Dunbar Moodie, who abused their mother Clarissa Meek so badly that after bearing seven children, she fled from the family home in Umzinto when she could take no more. With the help of friends, she sued Dunbar for divorce in 1876, a scandal in Victorian Natal. By the end of the court case that exposed his cruelty and lies, she was awarded the divorce "without a stain on her character". Clarissa – who must have been far from meek – supported herself by working as a governess on a Free State farm, and then as headmistress of the early St Cyprians College for Girls in Kimberley.

In 1877 her eldest daughter Charlotte visited her in Kimberley, and fell in love with Frederick Robert Moor (FR). In 1872, aged nineteen, he had set off from Estcourt in a wagon convoy with his brother

George and six farm workers, heading for the Kimberley diggings in the diamond rush. Joined by a third brother, they staked out and worked three of the original claims in the Big Hole.

Charlotte and FR married in Kimberley in 1878, when he sold his share of the claims to his brothers to buy a farm near Estcourt, following his father FW Moor into politics and farming. He served as a minister in successive Natal governments, rising to Prime Minister in 1906 and attending the conferences that led to Union in 1910, when they became Sir Frederick and Lady Moor.

The concerns of those bearded white Edwardian politicians centred on the bitter rifts between the English and Afrikaans communities caused by the Boer War. The moderate voices of John Tengo Jabavu, Rev John Langalibalele Dube, Solomon Tshekisho (Sol) Plaatje and others of the South African Native National Congress were ignored.

A little-known aspect of one of the final Union conferences was recorded by our aunt Shirley, FR and Charlotte's third daughter, who worked as his occasional secretary. On 9 March 1909 she wrote in her diary, which we found in a white attaché case after she died, and I published for the family:

> The question of the Capital has been a vexed one. They could come to no satisfactory agreement at the Conference, & it was finally left to the four Prime Ministers to decide. After a great deal of haggling, always between the Cape and Transvaal, Papa put a proposition to them, that we should have a new Capital altogether, on the Vaal at Vereeniging, where the treaty of peace was signed by Lord Kitchener & Botha. Botha fell in with the idea, but Mr Merriman objected strongly. However, as General Botha said, "It is the fairest proposition to everyone that there has been yet, & if Fischer agrees, you must come in on our suggestion". Mr Fischer however, who still hoped to get the capital in Bloemfontein, wouldn't stand in with Natal & the

Transvaal, & this present clumsy – & most expensive, I should think – arrangement of two capitals was come to.

Not to mention the judicial capital, Bloemfontein. Natal lost out and was mocked for decades as The Last Outpost.

FR served in the first Union government under Louis Botha, and since he spoke isiZulu like most Natal farm boys, became the senator representing 'Native interests' until 1920. In *Journey to Avalon*, Robert writes that despite the paternalist mindset of the times, FR was deeply concerned "for the well-being of Natal Africans".

In a powerful speech about African reserves in 1887, he chastised his fellow Natal legislators:

> We should really be ashamed of the condition in which these native locations are. There are no roads; there is no improvement ... I think that a great deal of this is the fault of the Government. If we had taken steps in the earlier days to open up these locations and introduce and foster the industries and trades of different sorts, we should have found these people in a far more progressive state than they are at the present moment.

A year later, writes Robert, FR again challenged the Legislative Council:

> How long are we going to keep these Natives in a state of barbarity that our laws crystallise them in? A day of reckoning must come, when this sort of thing must be faced and a solution must be found. I contend that until the Natives are put on an equal footing with the white people and the other settlers in this colony, so long we shall find our Natives being herded in their locations ... because we drive them to it.

A patronising colonist? Yes. But surprising in his foresight.

19

Because family myths often obscure facts, I am not sure if FR knew that his grandmother, Mary Ann Price, who was born in Bengal to a British father, James Price, had an unnamed Indian mother. She is the reason why, in these days of scrutinising family genetics as well as history, one of my daughter's ancestral blood profiles registers 1% Bengali.

The East India Company started trading in India in the early 1600s, and by the time of Mary Ann's birth in 1791, the British had muscled into large parts of the subcontinent. In those early days, they had to be pragmatic about men's needs, as few English women would venture to such a dangerous foreign place. Schools were created where the half-English daughters of Indian wives and mistresses could learn domestic arts and skills to prepare them for marriage to Englishmen in India.

At seventeen Mary Ann married Charles Sealy, an officer 20 years older, and in time bore him three daughters, though he was often away on military campaigns. During one of his prolonged absences, she fell in love with my English great-great-great-grandfather Lieutenant John Moor, who was only six years older. Even under the watchful eyes of other military wives in the cantonment, they went beyond dalliance and she became pregnant in 1819. Their solution was to elope to England on a sailing ship with her daughters. A fourth daughter was born 135 days out from Bombay, with John registered as her father.

While living in various places in England and France, often moving for fear of scandal, she and John had two more children. The vengeful Charles Sealy stormed back to England and sued John for damages of £1,000, an enormous sum that was paid by a childless mentor who protected the growing family. Charles died a few years later, so they could marry at last in 1826 and return to India.

Mary Ann had borne a total of twelve children before John died too, by then a Lieutenant-Colonel. After many vicissitudes back in England and strife with her surviving adult children, she emigrated to Natal in 1856 to join her youngest son, Frederick William (FW) Moor.

He had been attracted to settle in the colony in 1850 by the Irishman Joseph Byrne's description of a scheme devised with the help of the British Colonial Land and Emigration Commissioners. For a deposit of £1,000, Byrne became entitled to 5,000 acres of land in Natal, then issued a buyers' prospectus for lots of 20 acres in his Byrne Immigration Scheme, advertising widely in the British press and giving numerous lectures.

Here is a flavour of his purple prose fabricated to attract buyers – this from a man who had never visited Natal:

> Natal may be said to be unsurpassed in point of the salubrity of its climate by any other region of the earth ... droughts are unknown, pasturage ever plentiful, rivers innumerable ... ever flowing and watering all parts of the favoured land ... its wooded hills and grassy plains ... the summer is mild ... frost and snow unknown ... the soil is extremely fertile and capable of producing tropical plants and fruits ... its small white population is ever ready to welcome newcomers to share its prosperity.

The availability of a workforce was also emphasised:

> ... a main advantage Natal possesses over most other British
> Colonies is to be found in the large coloured population capable of
> field labour.

Byrne also assured potential buyers that Natal Africans were a body
of refugees with no prior claim over the land, who were simply
grateful for the protection that whites gave them. Lying conmen with
golden tongues and clever ideas for spending our money are ever
with us.

At nineteen, FW was persuaded to sign up with Byrne for 100 acres,
and paid for a cabin on the *Minerva*, which set sail on 27 April 1850.
After a rough voyage, she dropped anchor off Port Natal on 3 July.

Some of the passengers were taken off in surf boats, but heavy
seas that night drove the ship onto a reef at the Point, where it started
breaking up. All the passengers and crew were taken off safely the
next day, though their goods were either lost or washed ashore and
looted – including casks of rum supposedly guarded by the crew,
who instead got drunk on the unexpected bounty.

However, FW was well prepared and had taken out insurance,
done some basic medical training, and brought a medicine chest
which was rescued from the debris on the shore. He is also said to
have carried his future wife Sarah Annabella Ralfe ashore from a
surf boat after a shipboard romance.

Once at their Byrne destination, he built a small house to move
into after the wedding, then a more substantial house. Farming proved
difficult, however. Within a few years they left Byrne for Estcourt,
where he knew the land and climate were best suited for sheep farming. By then there was a first son and a new baby. FW was building
another new home when they had news that his mother Mary Ann
would soon arrive in Port Natal on the sailing ship *Annabella* –
which by extraordinary coincidence foundered on the sandbank at

the entrance to Port Natal harbour five years after FW's shipwreck. Again, there were no fatalities.

Stalwart Mary Ann thrived in Estcourt and pulled her weight by living to eighty-five, "a cherished granny still working at kitchen and sewing tasks in her farming community", as her great-great-great grandson Robert wrote in *Journey to Avalon*. The story I most enjoy about her is that she made her young grandsons join their sisters doing cross-stitch to keep them busy on rainy days.

20

One of those grandsons, Frederick Robert (FR), grew up to be serious and considered. Perhaps it was the attraction of opposites that drew him to marry the impulsive Charlotte Moodie.

She seems to have had energy to spare. Besides the usual activities of a farmer's wife, she had seven children and was a prolific writer of diaries, newspaper articles, two Boer War novels – *Marina de la Rey* and *Miss Vaughan* – short stories, sentimental Victorian poetry and songs. As a politician FR was often away on Government business, or on farming or constituency matters, and in his absences, she'd bundle the children by train down to the coast for holidays.

Their incompatible marriage soured over the years. In 1916 Charlotte bought the farm Ararat on which part of Umzumbe village now stands, paying £852 for "247 Acres 3 Roods 32 Perches of land", according to the deed of sale. There was no question of a divorce. Her grandson Donald in later years described this as "a perfect example of a civilised separation settlement".

She organised the building of a series of mud-walled holiday huts, with the biggest, Ballymuddle, for the family. When they were boys, Dad and Colin would lie on their stretchers watching snakes wriggle across Ballymuddle's sagging hessian ceilings, and he claimed that they'd hang onto cows' tails to cross the river when it was running low.

Next came a U-shaped brick farmstead, Craigievar, on a hill overlooking the river mouth, where her third daughter Shirley joined her to farm sugarcane and run a dairy.

Charlotte's grandchildren called her Momonie and remembered her fondly for her enthusiasm, which made them feel they were important to her. She met them when their train arrived at Umzumbe station, wearing a veiled hat and a long skirt, with her little dog Pamela by her side. They were allowed to run free all day before gathering around her at the piano after supper to sing. When it rained, they'd see her sitting up in bed writing poetry, holding a large umbrella overhead to ward off drips from the leaking tin roof.

As time went by, she subdivided part of the farm and sold off lots, giving some to her children. My grandmother Lena, her eldest daughter, received a beachfront site where Grandpa Owen designed and built an ingenious holiday cottage with irregular rooms that they called Eudaemonia (Greek for 'human flourishing').

Dad told us that it had a long-drop at the end of a walkway between amathungulu bushes, with a flag on a stake to show when it was occupied. You had to bang the structure with the stake to chase out any snakes before going in. That house is now a central part of the Pumula Beach Hotel.

Umzumbe village grew around the curly-eaved Edwardian station building and a little red-brick post office. In the Sixties, Dad and Colin were given a long narrow triangle of bush between the sea and the railway track, and our cottage was built in 1962 on Dad's section. You'd have to listen for the trains, pulled by puffing billies in the early days, before crossing the track to walk up to the trading store for newspapers, bread, liquorice ribbons, fishhooks and bait. A shoe-mender worked at his machine on the wide veranda with corrugated-iron rain tanks at each end.

That store and the passenger trains and the little station building are long gone, though until ten years ago our grandkids were still putting coins on the tracks to be flattened by the few goods trains that passed by, carrying crushed limestone to a cement factory in

Durban. Sadly the trains stopped running after the April 2022 flood damage, and grasses grow between the tracks now. It's a tragedy that this scenic railway has been allowed to deteriorate, especially as it carried passengers at low cost and could have been a tourist attraction.

Shirley never married and continued to manage what remained of the Craigievar farm until the late Sixties. She was a classic maiden aunt: kind, humorous, quietly clever, well read in history and politics and an expert farmer, with a fund of stories about South Africa's past. All her life she had a passion for Scotland and Scottish history, after falling for Major Robin Campbell when he marched into Maritzburg with the kilted Cameron Highlanders in 1906, during the Bambatha Rebellion.

We're not sure if she ever met this man she called "the Brigadier" in the journal she left among her papers; she tore out some of the pages so we'll never know the full story. After she died, we found another notebook with his photo and glued-in cuttings that showed she had followed his career for decades by subscribing to his regimental newspaper. He became one of the heroes of the First World War, married and had a family – all the dates annotated in pencil in her handwriting.

Born at a later time and formally educated, Shirley could have been a historian. Instead she farmed at Craigievar, read extensively, entertained visiting family and groups of friends, and when she could get away, insisted on travelling by midnight mail trains that arrived at dawn.

No visitor to her home on the hill could ever forget her china-blue eyes, lively conversation and long meals ending with bowls of creamy maas or pink amathungulu fool. She lived surrounded by books, Persian rugs, her dogs, her Jersey cattle – all their names beginning with D; the bull known as Dashing Daring Dauntless Desmond. And she'd shoot any snakes that weren't despatched by her foreman and protector, Mfayedwa Mtshali.

One day he used a dead mamba to show Owen and me how its curved needle-thin fangs sprang out and forward from its top jaw before it struck. He stroked underneath them with a stick and poison dripped onto the hot stone, a sizzling memory that is always in my mind at Umzumbe. However, the reptiles we see now are harmless green tree snakes, flickering striped lizards, and the ubiquitous geckos that scamper up walls and across ceilings, dropping hard little black and white poops everywhere.

For decades Shirley treated family and friends to holidays with a view over the Indian Ocean where the moon rose after happy days on the beach, and the Union Castle mail ship from Durban sailed past shortly after seven on Thursday evenings with all its lights blazing, heading for Cape Town.

Dad and Shirley and Mfayedwa died years ago, Craigievar has been demolished and the Union Castle line is no more. As our mothers used to say when things were finished, "All gone now. All gone."

21

The significant houses of my childhood like Craigievar have a powerful presence in different facets of the dragonfly eye, and sometimes crop up in my writing. As well as Woodcroft and the old house at Umfolozi, there was Grandpa Owen's Netherley, a rambling Edwardian home on Roberts Road overlooking the Maritzburg city centre. It had deep verandas on three sides, a greenhouse with dripping ferns off one of them, and a red-brick coach house at the back that had once housed a horse and carriage. Dad wrote of him:

> The Pater was full of initiative, could operate any & all machine tools, & his knowledge of steam engines was encyclopaedic.
>
> He had finished school at twelve, by which time he was proficient in short-hand and a talented pen & ink artist. At thirteen he bolted off to sea & spent two years under sail before the mast – rounded Cape Horn in a windjammer (the *Brenda*), sailed the roaring 40s and was set to pushing Ganges corpses off the bows of the ship while lying at anchor at Calcutta.
>
> When he got home from his years at sea, he worked in the coal mines managed by his father, studying mining survey at night school in Sheffield.
>
> On 12 October 1897, his twentieth birthday, he kicked over the traces and emigrated to South Africa. He surveyed the line for the telegraph from Stanger to Mbabane in about 1900 & the railway line to East Griqualand & the road to Estcourt, and helped to build the irrigation works at Weenen & Inkasini.

He served in the Boer War as an engineer of reconstruction on the Natal Govt. Railways, repairing the track, bridges & tunnels the Boers blew up. He saw the first Cavalry charge of the war by the 5th Lancers at Elandslaagte.

Ever ingenious, Grandpa Owen invented a process to extract tannin from wattle bark just before the First World War, which meant that a major Natal export took up much less space in cargo ships. As the war dragged on, so did the need for tanned leather for boots, saddles and Sam Browne belts. The tannic extract factory did well, and he sold his share to invest in other businesses.

His first wife Lena Moor, my grandmother, was the eldest of four sisters and adored by the family young. Her nephew Donald Moor wrote of her:

She was so natural and so friendly, so gay and full of life and original schemes, that she made life great fun ... There was never a dull moment when she was around with all her surprises – it was either a moonlight picnic, a Fancy Dress Ball or some other excitement or jollification. On her visits she never came empty-handed. Out of the car would pop a kitten or a home-made doll which she had already named. She made the world a happier spot, and I can understand her great love of Colin and Taffy.

In later years we learnt that her one failing was to be very much 'on top of the world' or 'down in the dumps', an unfortunate Moor failing.

Now I wonder how she got along with our dour Grandpa Owen whom she married at eighteen, probably to get away from the dull farm life expected of young society women then: visiting each other for tea and conversation, dressed up to the nines, with occasional trips to Estcourt.

Her tragedy was developing pernicious anaemia and starting to fade away. On medical advice, Grandpa sent her with her sister Shirley to an English nursing home run by a convent in Bovey Tracey, Devon. Her beloved boys, Colin and Dad, were parked at Blundell's, a nearby minor public school. Grandpa was too involved with his Natal businesses to sit with an invalid in England, so only Shirley was with her during her last days. She died towards the end of August 1921.

The head of the convent wrote a long letter to her mother Charlotte describing her final weeks, headed "All Souls Day":

> She was a good deal quieter and inclined to sleep those last few days and we hoped it was a good sign ... Her sister went into the room with the nurse ... she was lying very quietly when they saw a change come over her face and called back the Doctor and Father Saunders who immediately said the *last prayers* and she passed away! The boys arrived almost directly after – so you see it all took place sweetly and peacefully with the *right* people with her. She was very patient, but I think quite believed that she was getting better and going to sail for Africa in September ... The two dear boys felt it all very much and I regret that poor Mr Walters could not have been there.

The cause of pernicious anaemia was discovered a few years later: a deficiency of Vitamin B12, treatable with injections. The boys hurried home to their African lives as soon as they finished their schooling, rejecting the idea of further education.

Grandpa met and married his second wife Nita while in England on business. She had a fastidious taste for long slim skirts, dangly earrings, and fine things like Minton china and the Spanish silk shawl draped over her grand piano. She helped him choose Netherley and furnish it with antiques, large paintings in ornate gilded frames, and pleasantly mellow Persian carpets from a bale send out from Teheran after the First World War.

Only Dad and Colin knew that the impressive paintings were copies of works in British galleries, painted by her sister Ida Strother-Stewart, who was a copyist, a popular profession for women artists in the early 20th century.

Nita had bought a vargueno (Spanish or Portuguese writing chest on a stand) that was shipped out with furnishings they had chosen. It had its original iron fittings and handles, and inside the drop-down front were rows of small drawers with ivory columns and inlays, trimmed with red and gold. Dad inherited it among many lovely things after Grandpa died and Netherley was sold. I always liked the way its sombre severity concealed intriguing spaces, including a secret drawer.

When in time it came to me, I posted photos to the Victoria and Albert Museum in London, wondering about its age and care. Tim Miller of the Conservation Department hand-wrote a courteous letter explaining:

> … the chest itself is very likely to be 16th century or possibly early
> 17th century [Shakespeare's time!] … though the stand is more
> problematic … more often than not these are 19th century confections.

Later, after I'd written back to thank him and ask whether the ivory needed special attention, he wrote:

The vargueno (like most old furniture) was solidly and strongly made, and contact with people its raison d'ètre. Your vargueno is very much a *family* piece, which makes it infinitely more valuable than an object without that distinction ... I should adopt the cautious approach of accepting the ivory inlays as they are. This risks nothing.

The chest's cross and shell symbols show that it was dedicated to St Iago (St James). To imagine that it could have been taken by wagon on Camino de Santiago pilgrimages more than four centuries ago was reinforced when I saw a TV documentary about Spain mentioning a fable that St Iago was born in a field of stars.

There are little iron stars all round the vargueno's front edges.

Nita was vague and rather distant as she never had children. For all the Netherley abundance she was thrifty, buying seconds on sales for family presents and keeping them in a locked storeroom. The Netherley cook Anthony made delicious lemon juice and cakes that were scrumptious when fresh, though rock hard if there hadn't been visitors for a week or two.

An enormous Natal fig tree shaded the lawn in front of the house, and two stone lions strode across opposite plinths at the front steps, backed by lemon verbena bushes. Hunting trophies bristled on the veranda walls: horned buffalo and buck heads with brown glass eyes, and a warthog skull with tusks.

In later life, Grandpa Owen stopped shooting game and took photographs instead, with a camera he made from a discarded ammunition case. It used 120 rollfilm and he kept his negatives in a long wooden box chiselled NEGATIVES that was full of labelled brown half-envelopes.

Among them, our second daughter recently found a photo series of young women dressed Grecian style doing coordinated 'artistic' dances in the open air, and made prints. She tracked down their origin as members of the Margaret Morris Movement who visited South Africa in the Thirties, and discovered that the organisation still exists, so she was able to contact them. Grandpa Owen's photographs were printed in their next magazine, 75 years after he died.

He was a classic patriarch with strong views. David said he disliked frogs and remembered strolling with him round the Netherley garden in the evening with a spike on the end of his walking stick. Any frog they came across would be spiked and sent sailing over his neighbour's wall – anathema in today's eco-conscious era, but unsurprising for a tough old man who had made his own way in the world.

Christmas lunch on the widest part of the Netherley veranda was orchestrated by Anthony, dressed in crackling white cotton from his bald head with its round Gandhi cap to his immaculate white tackies.

As soon as Grandpa and Nita, our parents, uncle, aunt and cousins were seated, Anthony presented him with a silver tray holding an Elastoplast tin with his false teeth nestled on a bed of cotton wool. In fascinated silence we'd watch him insert them into naked gums and chew his mouth around until they felt comfortable, and lunch could begin. (I remember grandparents' dentures grinning pink-and-whitely from bubble baths of Steradent in glasses on their bedside tables overnight.)

Towards the end of the feast with turkey and all the trimmings, crackers and paper hats, Anthony brought out the flaming plum pudding which we kids loathed, though there was a consolation trifle. After extracting our loot of tickeys and silver charms from an obligatory slice of plum pudding, we'd shunt mouthfuls of it hand by hand under the table to David, the youngest among the cousins at the end, to flick into the lemon verbena bushes.

One of Netherley's attractions was a cavernous lavatory (too grand to be called a toilet) with piles of *National Geographic* on the intricately tiled floor, an invitation to linger. There was a high cistern and a long chain with a porcelain handle, though Grandpa later automated the seat so it rose up behind as you stood, releasing a nerve-racking deluge.

His workshop was in the former coach house across the back yard, a maze of pulleys that worked various machines – planes, lathes, drills – running off one motor. Going in there was like walking into a whirring Heath Robinson cartoon. He made a variety of fine furniture on those machines, including a tilting mirror with side pieces for each granddaughter when we turned twelve, a surprising gesture for an old man of his temperament.

As a former sailor, Grandpa could also sew – anything from his own shirt buttons to tents for taking his sons camping in the bush. There used to be a photo of him working the treadle of a venerable Singer as he stitched through a heap of canvas outside his workshop.

Generally dour, only once did he connect with Owen and me. He sang us a sea shanty in his dark study with its massive desk and shelves of engineering manuals, Conrad and Kipling, ending with a reminiscent smile.

The equally unforgettable Umfolozi home of our Norwegian grandparents and their loving warmth were a complete contrast to Netherley, which was demolished like most old houses in large gardens, and superseded by what Dad called a flock of bats.

Visiting Umfolozi village in the Nineties was a shock. The little station had vanished, along with the railway line, Lake Eteza – reclaimed for sugar farming – and the crocodiles. The house by the trading store looked smaller than I remembered, with a sad drought-stricken garden.

I've learnt not to go back to the places that linger in my memory.

22

At the end of 1950 after David was born, Grandpa summoned Dad to Maritzburg to run a metal die-casting business he'd bought.

My new school would be St Annes in Hilton – an exciting prospect, as reading about boarding schools had smitten me with dreams of dormitories and midnight feasts. Today it's considered posh, with an education never dreamt of in our time, but in the early Fifties it lagged behind Durban Girls College academically. After three terms of freewheeling in 4th Form, the headmistress Miss Wood summoned the parents to suggest pushing me up to 5th Form to make me put in more effort and work harder.

This meant an awkward term struggling to catch up with already-taught lessons and getting used to new classmates, though they were kind and welcoming. Survivors of the Class of '53 still keep in touch and occasionally the few of us left in Cape Town have lunch together to reminisce about our schooldays in the mist.

The dragonfly facets of those years shift to the Usherwood dormitories in the old main building; the ritual of 'Feet and Bottles' at the beginning of term with Sister Spaull in the San, when she checked our medications and inspected our feet for verucas (What? I'd never heard of the community affliction); the anarchic freedom of the 5th Form common room, a wood-and-iron shack off the gym where we relaxed from the stresses of school with gossip, speculation about boys, and Frank Sinatra and Nat King Cole on the gramophone. No one else was allowed in there, not even teachers.

There were inspiring English classes with excellent Miss Beggs –

humorous, long-chinned and nicknamed Bags. I sent her my first two novels decades later to thank her, sparking lively letters from England where Bags had retired, feisty as ever in her nineties.

The history teacher snapped one day that I was getting too big for my boots, so I gave up the subject for Matric to 'show' her, losing out on history that has taken me years to catch up. Do teachers realise the long-term effect of a caustic remark on a student?

In the gym, we heaved ourselves over the stolid jumping horse, balanced along the beam and swarmed up and down wall ladders. We were also taught Eightsome Reels and the Gay Gordons by the gym teacher, and danced with each other there on Saturday nights, teaching each other how to jive.

There were midnight feasts of condensed milk, jelly powder and the contents of tuck boxes, usually sitting on a roof adjacent to a window. In the dining room we stuffed ourselves with sausages and mash or meatballs like cannon balls. For pudding there'd be syrup mattress (a baking-pan-sized wodge of dense cake oozing with syrup), and chocolate mud with toenails (a similar-sized quivering chocolate blancmange scattered with desiccated coconut).

Of course there were salads and bowls of fruit too, but those giant puddings and the plates of fresh brown-bread sandwiches at tea between meals were eagerly consumed and, with luck, worked off by afternoon hockey or netball or tennis.

At the tables of mixed ages, the youngest diner would be asked to 'make a Moab' – a school custom of biblical origin which meant pouring water for a fingerbowl if we peeled fruit. Like all hallowed school rituals, it was probably used to confuse newcomers.

At weekends we'd walk around Hilton: to the Quarry with its brooding cliffs and rusty trolleys on old tracks, along the narrow tarred roads or daringly towards Monzali's, a secretive mansion rising out of a plantation across the main road. The Quarry was dammed and filled with water after my time at school, but it's impossible to forget our adventures there. Do rusty trolleys still lurk in the deep?

As a diocesan college, St Anne's had a daily chapel service when I sang alto in the choir, rewarded by rousing hymns and readings in the magnificent English of the King James Bible, though the pews were narrow and hard as we endured the hot-potato droning of Anglican clergymen. We attended the Church of the Ascension across the road on Sunday mornings too; I married there in 1959 and both our parents' ashes were stowed in its memorial wall when they passed on.

I wonder now if there is still an Ascension Day fête in the village? We'd make sure to be there in time for the gym routine by athletic boys in white vests and shorts, orchestrated by the legendary Hilton College PT teacher 'Pabby' Bould, and ending in a pyramid of eye-catching boyhood stacked with thrilling precision.

For school dances our dresses had to have sleeves and not be low enough, in the words of Miss Douglas, "to show the V of your bosom". For our Matric dance, I foolishly invited a Michaelhouse partner I fancied, only to spend the night watching my friends having fun while I had to deal with a Joburger who made it clear by sulking all night that I wasn't sophisticated enough for his ultra-superior self.

Some of us kept journals in hardcover exercise books, and we'd stick in snippets of each other's hair, annotated 'permed' or 'natural'. Tightly curled home perms were in then, though my hair had enough curl not to need one. These cringingly superficial journals of my last two school years record no profound thoughts, nor is there a hint of writing talent. I only wrote in them when something significant happened, recording hockey matches, outings, clothes, hikes and parties. They bulge with tickets, programmes, party invitations and memorabilia like shrivelled balloons and dead pressed roses, letters with early Fifties stamps, and all too few valentines.

'SWAK' written on the back of the envelope meant Sealed With A

Kiss. It's a trivial record compared with my granddaughters' insightful illustrated journals. I went through all the motions of a teenager, but the age gap of well over a year between me and my classmates meant that I was a green hometown girl under a veneer of know-how. (I should add that these banal journals came in useful for details when I wrote about teenagers of that time in *The Sweet-Smelling Jasmine*.)

Invitations for holiday parties overseen by vigilant parents came by card in the post. Boys wore school blazers and ties, and we our fullest skirts with stiff petticoats that flared out when we danced the London Jive, touching and twirling. It's called Swing now and was exhilarating when we boogied to Glenn Miller or The Inkspots. Mohair stoles kept us warm if it was a chilly night, shedding wisps on partners' school blazers.

Discreet lipstick and (eek) blue eye shadow were allowed by our mid-teens. Mascara came in black tablets you had to spit on before applying the gunk to your eyelashes with little brushes, leaving blobs that dissolved into black trickles down your cheeks if you sweated or cried. Cantankerous fathers yelled, "Go and wash all that muck off!" at made-up daughters trying to sneak out.

When I had a party at home, Dad requested a foxtrot, clutching me to his boep with a proud smile and advancing in a square around the edge of the floor. A tall redhead was the only boy who could waltz, which meant a few minutes' divine whirling if there was enough space.

Party catering was straightforward. Apart from Coca-Cola, innocuous punch, chips, peanuts and stuffed eggs, there'd be half a cabbage spiked like a hedgehog with toothpicks holding small chunks of cheese, red and green cocktail onions, and slices of gherkin.

Even with eagle-eyed host parents watching, boys would smuggle in a half-jack to spike the punch, or squashed packs of cigarettes for furtive smoking outside. There'd usually be at least one covertly showing off a well-worn condom packet. Nice Girls Didn't then for fear of falling pregnant. Girls Who Did made boys anxious. What we called FLs (for French Letters) had a notorious failure rate, and they were nervous of being saddled with a shotgun marriage.

Mothers warned daughters, "Always keep one foot on the floor." As if that would make a difference to determined teens.

Towards midnight, parents doing lifts would be at the door, peering into the last-half-hour darkness when things had at last got smoochy to *Goodnight, Sweetheart* or *I'll See You in my Dreams* before the lights were switched on at twelve by relieved hosts. Owen's trick during parties was to push stuffed eggs up exhaust pipes which resulted in pleasing explosions when people drove off.

I only realised what country hicks we were in Maritzburg when I was invited to Joburg for a week by a maverick friend. Having taken a demure party dress, I felt crushed by stylish teens wearing the latest American gear to jive and square dance. And they had waffles *for breakfast.*

At the end of our school years, two of us managed to scrape first class Matrics before heading into new lives, unaware of our boarding school naivety. I was sixteen going on seventeen when I started university – far too young, but confident I could handle anything.

Mum made my dresses and with her help I made some too. Learning to sew, knit, crochet, smock and embroider was expected of young women then, followed by how to make curtains for when we set up home. I could knit while reading or swotting, and later knitted a sweater for the University boyfriend I would marry. When our daughters arrived, I knitted and made clothes for them too, but disliked handwork which thankfully dwindled as they grew out of home-made clothes.

Now I wonder why these domestic labours prevailed for so long before I got down to serious writing.

From a later biography of one of our country's most admired writers, Bessie Head (*Bessie Head: Thunder Behind Her Ears* by a Natal University contemporary, Gillian Eilersen), I learnt that we were the same age. Bessie was born in Maritzburg, daughter of a white mother who had given birth to a baby of colour. Her mother was put into a mental institution and the family farmed Bessie out to foster parents. Later she was sent to St Monica's Home near Durban, from where she studied for a teacher's diploma.

St Monica's was one of the charities supported by my school house, Usherwood. Ever since reading that Bessie was there in 1952 when I'd visited with a teacher and some classmates, I've been haunted by the thought that she must have scorned us as unbearably patronising in our smart going-out suits with blue striped ties and black lisle stockings.

Her and my circumstances and life trajectories couldn't have been more different. Bessie's struggles were epic. After a few years of teaching, she became a journalist and anti-apartheid activist who left for Botswana on an exit permit. Leading an arduous exile's life with her young son from a failed marriage, she wrote her acclaimed books there before dying at forty-nine in 1986.

That life is neither fair, nor just, takes a long time to sink in.

23

There were war veterans among the 750 students on the Maritzburg campus of Natal University where I registered in February 1954. They lounged on the Union veranda spinning out delayed student years, smoking unfiltered Rembrandts as freshers like me scurried past, watching us with the hooded eyes of old gamblers who knew it all and pitied our ignorance.

Reading memorable books had made me think that perhaps I could be a writer one day. Reading newspapers made me think that maybe I could be a journalist. However, newspapers trained their staff on the job and in cadet schools then, and after Matric I was intent on university, where creative writing courses didn't exist.

The prevailing belief was that talented writers would find their own ways into print via publishers on the lookout for writing talent, and through good luck. Today, an agent is the usual route, and a knack for writing gory crime or dystopian horror stories is bankable.

But what do we know of our future needs, enthusiasms or careers when we leave school? At sixteen I chose English as my first major, and though there were some inspiring English lecturers, we didn't go further from the British canon than Alan Paton's second novel *Too Late the Phalarope*.

Varsity was a radical new world of lectures and tutorials, new ideas, deeper learning, being dazzled by professors and called "Miss Walters". I shared a ground-floor residence room in Lower Hags with my school friend Ann Donald (nicknamed Ducky at primary school after Donald Duck), and a brooding poster of Marlon Brando inside my cupboard door with his T-shirt sleeves rolled up, wearing a workmen's cap. He was still mesmerising decades later in *The Godfather*.

The curfew at Hags was 11pm, and our window was the traditional entry point for late-arriving seniors. We'd be woken at ungodly hours to unscrew the mesh burglar guard and let them in.

Most of us smoked a few cigarettes at parties to look sophisticated – Sobranie Black Russians with gold tips if we could afford them – and drank shandies or ginger squares, with a champagne glass of Grand Mousseux on special occasions. You soon learnt that too much would end in an unpleasant session barking into a big white telephone. Pineapple beer festered under our beds, and we toasted marshmallows over upturned radiators.

First years had to sit on stage in the Pietermaritzburg Town Hall in our undergrad academic gowns as a backdrop to the March 1954 ceremony where controversial Natal poet Roy Campbell received an honorary doctorate, and shocked the audience with a speech attacking the UK and the British Empire – anathema to Natalians then, as he well knew.

We had to wear those academic gowns for dinner every night, with grace said in Latin: *Benedictus benedicat per Iesum Christum Dominum nostrum, amen*, followed by frantic dabbing of inevitable spills on the black lapels.

On the first Rag Day, I blush to admit being in the pioneer squad of drum majorettes in home-made outfits with short white satin skirts, matching busbies and white tackies with white satin extensions to make them look like boots. On the second Rag Day I was bent over behind Ducky as the back legs of a Rag elephant made of wire and grey-painted fabric. (Maritzburg's isiZulu name uMgungundlovu means 'place of the elephant' and there is an elephant in the centre of the town crest.)

When Ducky was invited to join the group singing round braais where a senior, Ron Hobbs, played the guitar, she roped me in too. Shirley had given me Momonie's guitar on which I'd learnt a few basic strumming chords, so I joined with the guitar to sing *Stimela* and *Wimoweh, Cocky Robin, Daar Kom Die Alibama, The Golden Vanity, St James Infirmary,* and unrepeatable rugby songs.

It was romantic singing by firelight as we practised for Rag concerts, calling ourselves the Ragamuffins. Facing a Town Hall audience required fortification with Jerepigo or Old Brown Sherry beforehand – and 'O.B.s' remained the students' friend in my daughters' generation.

Lucky are women who meet a soulmate early – I was seventeen, Ron about to turn twenty-one – and hold him in their hearts all their lives. His twenty-first birthday present was the dinner jacket in which he took me to our first ball.

People today imagine the Fifties as a time of obedient doormat wives in full-skirted frocks and aprons and sleek men in suits, but those are movie stereotypes. He was a rugby-playing man among boys when we met, and our equal relationship was grounded on mutual respect. We fell in love in our safe campus environment during my second year, singing round braais, emotionally compatible despite different interests.

On the new psychometric tests we had taken before university, his abilities were equally balanced between science and the arts. He chose science and an MSc followed by a year of Chemical Technology in Durban, starting work as a chemical engineer and becoming an accomplished business leader unusually young.

Peering through the dragonfly eye at my carefree varsity years, the facets reflect lively lectures, challenging reading and absorbing pracs ... poetry that was new to me, like T. S. Eliot and the intricacies of Gerard Manley Hopkins ... being turned on to Shakespeare for life by the passionate lectures of Dr Peter Hey, who died some years later of war injuries he had suffered after being shot down over the Mediterranean.

There were daunting English tutorials with Professor Geoffrey Durrant, who only once praised an essay because I'd described Rosencrantz and Guildenstern as gormless. "How do you know that word?" he demanded. "From reading," I said feebly, aware that Kipling and war books wouldn't impress him.

My second major was Geography, and I also took a year each of Psycho, French and Zoology. Dissecting the frog *Bufo regularis* for a Zoo prac, the symmetry of its slippery innards and the strong pink muscles of its thighs gave me the first inkling of what attracted medical students to surgery, though it was dead and bloodless. Then there was the unforgettable chant to remember the sections of grasshopper legs: coxa, trochanter, femur, tibia and tarsus.

There were student pranks by men who went on to distinguished careers in academia, business, the arts, science and medicine, and nicknames carried over from school days: Prawn, Udwayi, Jags, Algae, Wiggy, Beeb, Pap, Little Pap his brother, and Bonk (which didn't mean then what it means now). My nickname at school had been Twig because I'd said, "Do you twig?" instead of "Do you click?" according to the school jargon. 'Twig' has stuck to me like a blackjack ever since with school contemporaries.

For sport, I played hockey and was captain of the Lower Hags rugby team for a match that lasted all of ten minutes. There were socials and dances between the lectures, tutorials, pracs, researching in the library, essays, and extensive reading. Life was busy and full.

Towards the end of every year, jacaranda blossoms popping under tyres at exam time is a sound that instantly transports me to sweating over questions in a hall of silent scribblers with a stalking invigilator.

My romance with Ron flourished as we walked entwined down

'the primrose path of dalliance' to Lower Hags, and on picnics by the uMsunduzi river under the willows – always with the whiff in his hair of the organic chemistry labs where he was researching for an MSc. I took forbidden rides around Scottsville on his second-hand Triumph 500cc motorbike, clinging behind him with my face hidden in case a family friend saw me and told Mum. While nursing at Addington she had dealt with the bodies of two motorbike riders whose heads had been ripped off.

After I took my driver's test in Mum's little navy Vauxhall – a matter of swotting up the rules of the road, driving round a few city blocks, stopping on a hill and smiling nicely at the examiner – she bravely lent it to us if Ron's father's Hillman Minx wasn't available for a night out. Once when he returned the Minx after some back-seat canoodling, his father asked him why there were white marks near one of the side back windows. I'd been wearing white shoes freshened up by tackie whitener. As my family says now in an expression of embarrassment, "Nye-heh".

24

The encompassing marquee of our white lives in early-Fifties Maritz-burg was seldom disturbed by politics, except for irate editorials in the newspapers about the increasingly restrictive new laws.

Anti-apartheid protests were only starting on white campuses as we headed for our finals in 1956, and were selective anyway. The Women's March to Pretoria on 9 August 1956 made no impression on campus that I was aware of, yet three months later in November, I was marching with a line of indignant students in academic gowns down Church Street in support of the Hungarian Uprising, when Khkrushchev sent Soviet army tanks into Budapest.

Other protest organisations flourished, then waned.

The Torch Commando was formed in 1951 by ex-servicemen in a spirit of wartime comradeship, with our RAF hero 'Sailor' Malan in the vanguard, supported by the United Party and other anti-Nationalists. Torchmen held dramatic processions with flaming torches on city streets, protesting against the removal of coloured voters from the voters roll in the Cape and crafty changes to constituency boundaries made by the new Nat government to keep themselves in power. Our uncle Colin wore a Torch Commando badge under his coat lapel which he'd flash at passers-by with a conspiratorial smile.

But the Torch flickered out in a few years as memories of wartime comradeship dimmed and ex-servicemen returned to their comfort-able white lives. Apart from pockets of Nationalists, Durban and the Midlands were staunchly United Party.

A courageous exception was our neighbour at home, Liberal Party chairman Peter Brown, who was continually harassed. We'd see sunlight glinting off the binoculars of security policemen sitting on the hillside above us, watching his house. Despite his wife Phoebe sitting on his papers when they were raided, he was jailed several times for months.

The Anti-Republican League was a milder version of the more radical Horticulturists who packed Nat meetings and sprayed the audiences with fire hoses. In Natal, there were Freedom Radio broadcasts of anti-Nat propaganda, with interludes of *God Save the Queen*.

Dad put up a flagpole to fly the Union Jack in front of our new home in Montrose above the winding main road (now the N3); he said it was there to annoy Nationalist ministers driving past. Later he told us it was one of the antennae relaying Freedom Radio broadcasts transmitted from a van being driven around, as the security police didn't have the technology to locate them.

More seriously, there was talk of sabotage by angry English-speaking servicemen forced out of the army and local governments in favour of Afrikaners.

My future father-in-law Bertie Hobbs was a decent, quiet man who had followed his father into the South African Police. Eber Launcelot Hobbs had been an English sergeant and a saddler with the Imperial Yeomanry who came to fight in the Anglo-Boer War and stayed. In 1960 Bertie was forced to resign from his office job after decades of police service, having been ordered to move to Pretoria within three days – which would have meant leaving the home he had lived in with his family for more than 30 years.

It was a classic example of how public services were clearing out the *Engelse* to make way for Afrikaners, a tactic repeated today by our current government for their cadres. The protests fizzled out or went underground as ANC members, Liberals and Communists were banned, hunted and jailed, while the Nationalists grew more powerful as people flocked to vote for them at the polls.

White life was comfortable, and apathy ruled.

Central Maritzburg was beautiful: mellow red-brick Victorian buildings, pantiled roofs, verandas with intricate encaustic floor tiles in cream and russet and black, and citizens ambling down the lanes running between the main streets.

By contrast, the caravan that became Twiggie's Pie Cart had slumped into the tarmac in a corner of the Market Square parking lot, and was the only place in town for late-night fast food. Patrons from law students to labourers to night-shift reporters on *The Natal Witness* stood shoulder to shoulder at the counter. Twiggie was as famous for his surly impartiality – first come, first served, barking orders at his cooks – as he was for leaning over the counter to leer at girls, getting more and more sloshed as the night went on.

My version of the Jacobsen nose made me self-conscious for years until the night he leant over the daggy counter and said, "You've got the cutesht little noshe I ever sheen." I wrote about him and three fictional ex-servicemen who meet there in my post-Second-World-War novel, *Kitchen Boy*:

> They met on Friday evenings at Twiggie's Pie Cart in Market Square ... reading each other's faces in the light spilling from the serving hatch where Twiggie ruled until the early hours of the morning, yelling irritable orders at the cooks sweating in the galley. "Mixed grill! Hoddog! Pie and hotters! Beans on toast! Cowboy breakfast!"
>
> When the heaped plates with still-sizzling chips were handed down – "Here you are, cock. Okay?" – they'd stand along the counter and bolt the food, then gulp down cups of coffee, making small talk before separating with muttered goodbyes ...

Now Kenneth sits recalling the pie cart and the light bulbs
dangling above the steamy cave where Twiggie presided, sultan of
the hungry on Maritzburg nights.

Apart from Peter Brown, fellow Liberals and protesting students,
white political activism in Natal was minimal then. The brutal forced
removals from Sophiatown, District Six and communities of colour
all over the country awakened some consciences. The Black Sash was
founded in 1955 and the Progressive Party in 1959 – starting with a
manifesto that included a qualified vote (radical at that time).

But most South African whites kept their blinkers on and enjoyed
their inherited comforts for the next three decades. At universities,
most of us were too busy being students to notice what was happening under the pleasant surface of our suburban lives in the Fifties.
We must have been the last generation for whom the future and a
range of available jobs beckoned like the yellow brick road in *The
Wizard of Oz*.

Dropping out or taking a gap year weren't options. We worked
hard, partied sometimes, and graduated in the post-war boom, committed to steady jobs and raising families in homes we could afford
if the breadwinner earned enough to pay interest on a bond. We
furnished them with hand-me-downs and from sale rooms, saving
up for Big Things like fridges.

Though I devoured newspapers and books, considered myself
politically aware and despised the Nat politicians with their trembling
fern-and-carnation buttonholes, I also wore blinkers. Our lives were
only ruffled by black employees who needed signed permissions in
their dompasses or help with family problems.

My real education began when I emerged in the late Sixties from
my baby-oriented years, became involved with a farm school, started

freelance writing and later became features editor on a new magazine for black women, *Thandi*.

Increasing contacts with people in different communities led to a deeper understanding of the endless insults and traumatic pain of apartheid, of our shameful past, and in too many respects, of our continuing present.

Student life ended when Ron and I graduated in the Class of 1956 – he for the fourth time after a post-MSc year of Chemical Technology in Durban, me with a lowly BA. He was keen to start work as a chemical engineer and earn a living after six years of university funded by bursaries, and had left for Joburg by the time I sailed away on my long-planned odyssey.

During our fervent goodbyes, I had asked him please to wait for me while I got the yen to travel out of my system. He roared off on the Triumph to his first job and digs in a Parktown North back yard, resigned but sceptical. We hadn't discussed anything long term and I wasn't ready to settle down. It was a big ask, though, and unfair.

25

On 4 April 1957 the *Carnarvon Castle* eased away from the Durban quay in a blare of foghorns and multi-coloured streamers falling on friends and relatives waving below. My leaving attire was a light grey suit with a nipped-in waist and pencil skirt, a perky little turquoise hat with a net, black suede gloves and a black patent leather handbag.

The Union Castle Tourist Ticket for a 12-day voyage to Southampton was a graduation present. There was also an advance twentieth birthday present of a set of red leather-veneered suitcases lined with moiré taffeta: two suitcases, a matching vanity case and a hatbox with shoe pockets. My portable typewriter and books went into the hatbox with a few pairs of shoes. My only hat was on my head.

In hindsight, the leaving finery and cumbersome luggage must have been due to Mum's unfulfilled dreams of travel. Whatever her reasons, they made me feel as though I was on the brink of glamorous adventures.

Not yet, though. The tourist berth was steerage in a hot five-bunk cabin shuddering above the engine room, shared with four unknown young women. Despite initial seasickness while 'the mailboat' plunged giddily down the Wild Coast, we became friends as the sea calmed down and we steamed on.

Voyaging was a new world of shipboard activities and many-course meals, stopping off at ports along the way – East London, Port Elizabeth, Cape Town, Las Palmas – for brief expeditions. There were mock Crossing the Line ceremonies round the pool and a captain's cocktail party. Couples cuddled in shady corners of the deck. Dolphins curved away with the bow waves. The stars at night were never so bright.

In the Bay of Biscay before docking at Southampton, we cabin mates signed our names on a dinner menu, added my great-aunt Marjorie's London address, stuffed it into an empty wine bottle, jammed in the cork and threw it overboard.

To our astonishment, the menu turned up a few months later, forwarded with a letter from the British Embassy in Paris. It had been fished out of the sea at Finisterre by the magnificently named Monsieur Jean-Louis Bramoulle Kergoff en Plouguerneau. He probably hoped for a reward, though all we could afford was a swanky English postcard via the British Embassy with *"Merci beaucoup, Monsieur"* on the back and our signatures.

The voyage to England had another purpose besides a brief secretarial course to back up the touch-typing skills I'd learnt from *Teach Yourself Typewriting* for my university essays. I was in the second wave of family young despatched to Marjorie to have, in her view, our rough colonial edges smoothed off.

For three months she put me up in a garret at Mrs Mac's boarding house, just round the corner from the Paddington hotel she had created and owned. Since she had been alerted by preceding cousins that I was putting on airs about achieving the first degree in the family, I was under scrutiny and had to earn my way into her esteem before starting work, finding somewhere to live and earning enough to travel.

Marjorie was the youngest Moor daughter, as vivacious and energetic in her sixties as she had been as a prizewinning schoolgirl at Wykeham in Maritzburg. When the First World War broke out, she was in Scotland volunteering as a social worker in the Leith slums near Edinburgh. She enlisted as a cook with the Scottish Women's

Hospitals in France and worked in a field kitchen near the front line before being commissioned into the WAAC (Women's Auxiliary Army Corps, formed in 1917 because of the growing shortage of military men). In Dad's fond memoir about The Aunts:

> She served at the Catterick camp where she commanded 500 rather tough women, aged herself only twenty-three, and at war's end was put in charge of demobilising 800 servicemen. Awarded the MBE, she worked for a time as editor of the National Liberal Party's magazine until Lloyd George's coalition broke up, then began her hotel career as manageress of a London hotel.

With so many men lost in two wars, go-getting women like Marjorie stepped into the gaps. She had drive, chutzpah, and a large circle of friends, remaining single all her life, though there were lovers. After several years' hotel experience, she created Miss Moor's Hotel in two houses at 10-12 Craven Hill, the respectable end of Praed Street in Paddington, and close to Hyde Park. It catered for South Africans 'who longed for a feel of home amid the fog and cold of London'.

During World War Two she battled on as a residential HQ for people from the Ministries, the Admiralty and the War Office, spending many nights on the roof as a fire warden during bombing raids: "We lost windows, ceilings, walls, and rooms were thick with dust during the Blitz. I had only nine employees. I was up to my ears in debt. But somehow we scraped through," she told an interviewer on a post-war visit home. In 1953 she was the only woman among 18 British hoteliers who went in a delegation to America to learn how hotels were run there, examining "everything from basement kitchens to attics in forty hotels from the Waldorf Astoria to tiny roadside hotels".

Gaining Marjorie's respect took time. After stints of helping in her hotel dining room, followed by tears of protest at being labelled in advance as stuck up, she accepted that it was sabotage by two preceding cousins and we got on well. Her rough-edge-smoothing was confined to pronouncing place names – eccentric village names are one of the delights of the English countryside – and correcting my Damon Runyon-speak, common currency at varsity then.

Locally based cousins and I were invited one by one for weekends at her country retreat, the 17th century Clock House that had been the gatehouse to partially burnt-down Merton Hall near Thetford in Norfolk. She rented it as a friend of the De Grey family, several of whom had visited her parents in Natal when her father was Prime Minister. Walking around that beautiful estate was like going back in time to sylvan England, as De Grey forebears were granted it after taking part in the Norman conquest. There were Saxon barrows and Merton is in the 1086 Domesday Book. A large portion was handed to the British Army during World War Two.

Marjorie took me to lunch once with Lord Walsingham (formerly Lieutenant-Colonel George de Grey) and his wife Hyacinth, who confided at the table that she was a witch. Since she seemed more like a well-off countrywoman than a caster of spells, it was the first "Huh?" moment of many as I groped my way through British idiosyncrasies.

In a crowning gesture of acceptance, Marjorie invited me as her partner to the annual British hoteliers' gala dinner at Mansion House in the City. In a long dress borrowed from a friend, I stood in a semicircle of courtly gents wearing white tie and tails in one of London's grandest historic buildings, chatting before a lavish banquet.

For three months at a secretarial college on the Bayswater Road, I learnt shorthand and sped up the touch typing that over the years has been my most useful skill as a writer, allowing me to transmit thoughts to print almost as fast as I think. Shorthand was a waste of time as it was soon replaced by recorders. My portable typewriter was useful for a weekly aerogramme to the family, with a carbon copy for Ron with hand-written endearments. Mum kept and filed all her letters, so I have an unexpected diary spanning most of 1957 and 1958.

In my spare time from the college and revelling in London, I wrote short stories for magazines. In the heyday of short story and science fiction magazines, it was the classic way for young writers to get a foot on the literary ladder, but my feeble efforts were all rejected and petered out.

While full of confidence at twenty that I could deal with most challenges, I still hadn't encountered real life beyond the prostitutes on the Bayswater Road at night – and being mistaken for one on a foggy evening walking back to Mrs Mac's in a new blue raincoat and heels. I turned and hissed "Footsack!" and the man sheepishly melted away.

At the end of the course, I borrowed our Estcourt cousin Malcolm Moor's bike and cycled down to Cornwall, invited by John Morgan, my neighbour at Mrs Mac's, to stay with his family on his return home to St Austell. Cycling alone was safer then and the youth hostels along the way were friendly. I was hosted for a week by the Morgans and driven all over that craggy peninsula in John's open MG, an exhilarating break from typewriters.

If he'd hoped for romance, he was far too shy to make an approach, and I was just glad to have made a friend who shared his MG and Cornwall with me.

26

After cycling back to London, and two indifferent temporary jobs with advertising companies near Fleet Street, the spectre of more office work loomed. The sole highlight of the temp jobs had been two copywriters Cossack-dancing to present their latest slogan: "There are NO holes in No-Holes Tasty Bread".

Then I heard on the Earls Court grapevine that the London County Council needed supply teachers, and accepted graduates without a teaching diploma. It paid more than office work: 56 shillings (nearly three pounds) a day, which meant I could save up to travel. Better still, Commonwealth citizens working in Britain didn't have to pay income tax if you left within two years.

In the old LCC building diagonally across Westminster Bridge from Parliament, I was X-rayed for TB, interviewed about my education, and asked to produce my Matric and BA certificates. Once cleared, I learnt that my assignments would be to secondary modern schools in the Borough, Elephant and Castle and Lambeth districts – tough areas then, south of the river.

The easy acceptance and good pay were soon explained: filling in for usual teachers meant keeping unruly kids occupied so they didn't make too much noise. In the anarchy of their classrooms and Cockney chatter, I learnt about crowd control and to talk about Africa instead of teaching, leaving my mistakes behind when I moved on to the next school.

"Why aincha black then, Miss?" was always the first question when I walked into a class.

The secondary moderns were light years away from the disciplined schools I had attended. The teenagers were cocky, streetwise and swore like navvies, and I had to fudge my ignorance of two of the subjects I was supposed to teach (bookkeeping and ballroom dancing) though I could show them how to do the London Jive. Many of their fathers worked 'dahn the docks' if employed at all, though one girl's father had gone up in the world: his job was to pull the lever that raised and lowered the Tower Bridge bascules. From a later-published short story, *The Happiness of Annie Watts*:

> The girls in my class were nearly fifteen, dawdling through their last few terms at school and alien to the neatly uniformed schoolgirl I had been. They wore the latest tacky fashion sold in the street markets, fluorescent sweaters and tight black skirts, and teased their back-combed hair into towering beehives whose degree of fuzziness showed how many nights they had been slept in. They squeezed their feet into winklepickers with worn-down spiky heels that made thousands of dents in the wooden classroom floors. Their only form of exercise was tottering for the bus.

Sometimes kids would be absent because their families were on a Kent farm picking hops – "'op-pickin" – and partying with other pickers in the evenings. In the winter months it was dark and cold when I left for work, and still dark and cold when I made it back to the rented house on Holland Road shared with four friends. But the pay was good and the Commonwealth teachers I met were a bonus. We'd exchange tales about our different lives over sandwiches in the staff room at lunchtime.

The worst part of supply teaching was lunch duty, a gruelling ordeal with canteen food slopped on plates, sitting with children who seldom washed. Angry mothers would stomp into the schools to throw punches at a teacher they thought had misjudged their little Alfie or Flo. And the Nit Lady came every term with a fine-tooth steel comb to check the kids for hair lice and nits, though today – oh irony! – even Top School kids get them.

In 1959, E. R. Braithwaite from British Guiana, who had come to Britain to fly with the RAF during the Second World War, published the bestseller *To Sir With Love*, based on his experiences as a black teacher in London's East End. Sidney Poitier played his part in the subsequent movie. My scruffy copy of the book did the rounds of supply teaching friends, and I had the privilege of meeting him years later when he came to give a talk at our daughters' school, and to have him sign it.

More recently, the BBC series *Call the Midwife* brought back visceral memories of that time and place: teeming docks, Fifties and early Sixties hit songs, pub brawls, wives in aprons scrubbing doorsteps, snot-garbled kids' talk, retro clothes, winklepickers clacking on wooden floors, and those beehive hairdos.

When I arrived in the spring of 1957, London still had bomb craters where rows of houses had been destroyed during the war, their rubble softened by weeds that included the tangled flowering creeper London Pride. Municipal gardens blazed with squadrons of red and yellow tulips. Barrow boys chaffed passers-by from fruit and vegetable barrows on the pavements with signs like "Don't squeeze me till I'm yours". The cathedrals and art galleries and blissful museums were free.

Socialising with friends at bottle parties took up occasional evenings when I wasn't visiting worldly Marjorie, or writing letters, or working on a new story. Friends and I bought standing tickets or seats in the gods to see plays and musicals and ballet and rousing concerts in the Albert Hall.

Mum's closest brother Jake, on a business visit from Joburg, took three of us to Drury Lane to see *My Fair Lady* with Julie Andrews and Rex Harrison – from the royal box, the only last-minute tickets available. It had a retiring room with a flunky in knee breeches, pink stockings and a white wig. Jake called us his harem as he swept us off to the Berkeley Hotel for dinner.

He had earned his MSc by walking miles to and from Wits University for night classes, then suffered lung damage in a factory making mustard gas that had been requested by the British Army in World War Two, but never used. The barrels were dumped off the coast of East London after the war. Jake lived to ninety-one with bubbling half-lungs, writing a new verse of a love poem to his wife Rhona every birthday after she died. They had eloped when she was eighteen.

On occasional weekends, I was warmly welcomed by the Eustace family in Sevenoaks. Dad had kept in touch with his school friend Bob Eustace and I began a lifelong friendship with his daughter Jane after spending the first Christmas with them, including beagling on Boxing Day. Beagling is like a fox hunt on foot: you plod across the countryside following a pack of baying beagle hounds chasing rabbits. Nothing much happens – I didn't see them catch one – but the crisp winter air sharpens your appetite for lunch with a sherry.

A great treat was being swept with Jane along country roads to a ball in Bob's open-top 1930s Bentley, when those Saturday nights in the school gym paid off, as I knew how to dance the Gay Gordons and Eightsome Reels. Another of Dad's school friends was a stockbroker who took me to the viewing gallery of the London Stock Exchange.

Memories of the late Fifties in London crowded in when I wrote in my eighth novel, *True Blue Superglue*:

London was the centre of the world then, a dazzling force-field. South African friends arrived to spend a few nights sleeping on our sagging sofa while they looked for jobs and their own digs, all of us dizzy with the exhilaration of working in a fabled city. Our social life revolved around coffee bars with hissing espresso machines, cupboard-sized Chinese restaurants and bottle parties where we sat on floor cushions, drank plonk and dunked bread rolls in our soup. A special night out meant a convivial din of folk singers and guitars in the Troubadour.

Checking if the Troubadour is still there, I read that it was established in 1954 and is now 'a historic live music venue'. Historic? I'd turned seventeen that year.

London was all adventure, from Chinese eateries to coffee bars and skiffle bands with metal thimbles hammering on washboards, from Covent Garden's fruit, veg and flower market to the highest gods at nearby Drury Lane, from The Prospect of Whitby pub downriver flanked by Wapping warehouses to the abundant Hyde Park trees in summer and the tube trains thundering underground.

Sometimes on my way home, I'd take a red bus from Parliament Square, up dignified Whitehall, skirting the edge of Trafalgar Square, towards Piccadilly Circus, past Eros and Swan & Edgar department store into stately Regent Street, then through Oxford Circus to bustling Oxford Street, Marble Arch, the Bayswater Road and Paddington – so many of the names on our Monopoly board.

Walking with friends in the evening along the Thames embankment, we'd stop to watch the river gliding in liquorice twists under the bridges as Big Ben chimed, or backing up past the Houses of Parliament as the tide came in.

It was in London that I learnt the particular value of walking city streets – either alone or later, in foreign cities, with a guide. You notice details like an indulgence of seafood on crushed ice in a window or a row of old plates in familiar patterns on a street market table. The expression of a busker playing a joyful violin, his cap gaping on the pavement for coins. The irresistible aroma of fresh bread from a bakery. Little girls swishing their dresses as they walk. A street sweeper humming a tune.

Over the next six months there were more extensive travels when someone had access to a car.

Sitting on one of the fallen monoliths at Stonehenge with no one else in sight, I thought of druids and *Tess of the d'Urbervilles*, which had been a setwork. Photographing Tintern Abbey in the dreamy Wye Valley: ruined walls, sunlight slanting on mossy stones, cows cropping lush grass where the nave used to be. In Cambridge I went punting and had earnest conversations with students I'd jived with at teenage parties. Jane and her brother John drove me down to Tiverton in Devon in a 1928 Alvis to visit Dad's old school, Blundell's – where I found 'Taffy Walters' carved inside a cupboard in his former boarding house.

It must have been a very sad time for him, as he and his brother knew that their mother Lena was being treated unsuccessfully for pernicious anaemia in a nearby village.

27

During a school holiday I took the Norseman train from Kings Cross to Newcastle docks, then a steamer over the choppy grey North Sea to visit relatives in Norway.

As the first South African granddaughter to return, I was fêted at family dinners where each person would *skål* me separately with aquavit that required reciprocating. Though I learnt just to wet my lips, the liquid hospitality had me reeling off to sleep under a crisply sheeted feather *doona*.

It was a rare privilege to walk streets in Bergen and Arendal where my ancestors had walked, and to meet Bestemor's chuckling old sisters, Tante Tina, Tante Monda and Tante Alla, who were so like her.

In Norway my dragonfly facets glow in the red and blue of the flag that far-flung Norwegians display on a little silver stand in their homes. Brimming baskets of blueberries and raspberries in street markets. *Rømmegrøt* lovingly made: heated and thickened sour cream served with melted butter, berries and cinnamon. Rainbow battalions of *smørrebrød* (open sandwiches), super-fresh cod, *labskaus*, crusty butter-fried *fiskeboller* – and the brown yuckiness of *gjetost* (goat cheese), which at least I tried.

Remembering to say *Takk for maten* ("Thanks for the meal") after every repast. Walking under the ancient timbers of the medieval Fantoft stave church built like an upside-down Viking ship and reconstructed near Bergen. Zooming cross a fjord in a small boat towards painted wooden holiday homes on an island, then down the coast on a double-hulled hovercraft to Stavanger, then Arendal.

A week later in Oslo, I stood in awe of the size and elegance of an excavated *Vikingskipet* (Viking ship).

With Norwegian generosity I was showered with gifts: a snowflake-yoked sweater, enamelled teaspoons, family silver and a wooden nutcracker with a carved face under a floppy red hat. Carvings like this were whittled by young men hiding in the mountains from the Nazis during the Second World War occupation. Prominent on a wall in Tante Kristiane and Onkel Otto's house on an island near Arendal was a photograph of a Nazi general surrendering to a young Norwegian private at the end of the war.

Norway was hard to leave, though I was able to return briefly with Mum in 1970.

After a first year of supply teaching in London, cousin Malcolm and I hired a Morris Minor big enough for four (at a squeeze) to explore 'The Continent'. We signed up a Benoni couple who'd advertised for a shared car at the Overseas Visitors' Club in Earls Court.

The four of us set out with a trunk on the roof rack holding two canvas tents, four airbeds, sleeping bags, cooking equipment and basic rations like tea, rice and oatmeal, to be supplemented by markets along the way. For nine weeks we camped and youth-hostelled around Europe, visiting fabled cities and landscapes still recovering from the war. The museums and galleries and cathedrals were free and sometimes empty, as there were few tourists.

There were signs of war everywhere: bullet-scarred walls, ruined buildings, cracked streets, bomb craters. But normal life had started again in thriving street markets displaying fresh cheeses and prepared seafood, sizzling sausages, abundant fruit – and *Weinstubes* along side roads where we could taste and buy wine made from nearby vines. I remember still the lovely array of vineyards, apple blossom and half-timbered homes in the Ahr Valley, which was devastated two years ago by tumultuous flooding.

It soon transpired that Mr and Mrs Benoni were on their honeymoon, preferred Coke to wine, and were not interested in museums or art galleries or cathedrals. Relieved to be temporarily free of them, we went our separate ways at destinations. I'd scribble notes every evening by lamplight to supplement the few transparencies I could afford to take on the new 35mm Kodak Retina IIIc camera I bought in Cologne for my twenty-first birthday, and used for decades before giving it recently to a camera-fundi grandson, who continues to use it.

There were vast fields of tulips in Holland – blazing red, yellow, pink – giving way to canals and lace-makers in the doorways of Bruges ... a visit to the Atomium in Brussels (recently built for the 1958 World's Fair) ... walks in the Black Forest where Rumpelstiltskin could have popped up at any moment ... a quick dip in a Swiss lake ... clopping through Vienna in a carriage ... and on through the Dolomites to Italy.

We could spend a night in a youth hostel if we hid the car round a corner, and were able to avoid campsites except in cities. It was okay then to camp on an open space near a road, though there were hazards.

One early evening we pitched the tents on a promising site at Aquileia near Venice, only to be woken next morning by a horde of biting ants. We'd camped in the ruined cloister of a basilica sacked by Goths. Packing up fast, we hotfooted to the car over the remains of a Byzantine mosaic floor and drove on.

Italy was a cornucopia of delights and surprises where we wandered along quiet Venetian canals, venturing into empty churches, and viewed the ancient buildings with mossy skirtings from a vaporetto (gondolas being too expensive). In Murano, I bought a necklace of translucent blue glass beads for the equivalent in lire of two rands, and wear it still. We shopped in markets for buckets of pink cooked shrimps, crisp morsels of whitebait, bowls of glistening olives and fresh crusty rolls, the creamiest of ice creams and the fruitiest of granitas. Station cafés had sensational (and affordable) pasta.

A spectacular campsite with a view over Florence like a painting gave way to the Via Appia near Rome and a walk among ancient skulls and bones lining musty catacombs. In Pompeii, we saw the centuries-old agonies of writhing plaster bodies cast in the spaces left by people dying in the ash-fall. Everywhere, mottled feral cats could be seen slinking through the ruins.

A few nights on, camping in a field near Naples, three grizzled older men materialised out of the dark with bent shotguns over their arms. We exchanged nervous glances ... could this be the Mafia? In trepidation, we invited them to have a drink with us and Malcolm fetched the straw-covered flagon of Chianti from the car. Bingo! They had been prisoners of war in South Africa, and seeing our flag on the car, wanted to tell us how good people had been to them.

Travel is humbling as you learn how wrong first impressions can be.

Bypassing Florence as we drove north, we crossed the French border and took the coast road to Marseilles to drop off the teetotalling Benonis, who were leaving us to fly home, probably to their relief as much as ours. Then it was south again towards Spain via Avignon and Aigues-Mortes on a wild and windy night, where we turned off to an ideal camping spot on the grassy bank of a small river. Next morning we washed our laundry in the river, drying everything on bushes in the sunshine before crossing the Spanish border to the Costa Brava and a crystal-clear swim in a quiet cove bristling with deserted gun emplacements.

Tossa was a lovely little village teeming with holidaymakers and tourist shops, so we were soon back on the coastal plain to Barcelona through long avenues of trees and hayfields with oxen pulling farm carts, heading for a recommended bullfight.

The red-brick bull ring had cement seats where we had to hire leather cushions. At 5.30pm sharp the band started playing as the matadors and toreadors entered in a vivid procession: lithe men in tight black breeches, boleros glittering with gold braid and swirling deep-pink capes, followed by horses jingling with bells.

My travel journal has a long description of the evening which is undeniably dramatic for a Sunday, but the bloody teasing of the bulls and their killing is brutal, with a baying crowd that mocks and boos poor performers. Afterwards we drove around the quiet Barcelona streets with open windows, searching for an open space where we could breathe again.

Choosing a camping space at dusk is not a good idea. This time we pitched the tent in a flat open place with a high rock wall, so stony that we could hardly knock in the tent pegs. Next morning early sunlight was flickering on the tent walls when there was a cough outside and a man gesticulating for us to leave, *Pronto pronto!* We had camped in a quarry where they were about to dynamite another section of rock. Again we dismantled and fled.

That day was warm and clear. We stopped for a swim in a beautiful little bay and when evening came, decided not to pitch the tent but choose a space for our sleeping bags between two beach dunes. It was an even bigger mistake. We were accosted and moved on by two Guardia Civil cops brandishing torches and truncheons. "Drug smuggling is big business along that coast," we were told at the next youth hostel.

Among the almost-deserted beaches along this coast was a bay sweeping towards the jutting cliffs of the Peñon de Ifach, where we lingered to take a photograph. All those beaches must be crowded now with roasting holidaymakers. How lucky we were to travel then.

The shortest route to Gibraltar on the map ran from Alicante via Murcia. As the twilight darkened, we shuddered over rutted gravel roads, every now and again threading through huddled villages with lamplit shops where shadowy people traded as they must have done in the Middle Ages. I felt as though we had gone back in time that night. The road seemed deserted, so we decided not to pitch the tent but slept uncomfortably in the car, heads on our sleeping bags.

Gibraltar was a trumpet-call from Britain with Union Jacks drooping on navy vessels in the harbour, and familiar buildings at the foot of the mighty rock. We climbed up past scrambling apes to venture through dank tunnels ending in cannons and a hazy view of Africa across the Straits.

At our next stop Granada we took an evening walk up a road past caves with dancers in whirls of bright frills gyrating to sensuous guitars, and slender men in black clicking their heels to castanets. The cave dancing was too expensive for campers on a tight budget to enter, but looked like mini carnivals from the dark.

Most memorable were the long still pools of the Alhambra early next morning, photographed through intricate Islamic arches without anyone in sight. Their timeless tranquillity remains forever in my mind's eye, and on a few transparencies in a basement slide box. We drove on through Portugal and lovely Lisbon, followed by a not so lovely meal of tough goat meat ... then stretches of Spain and France again to Paris, where we could pitch our tent in the official campsite in the Bois de Boulogne.

Travelling with Malcolm was a pleasure because we were interested in the same things; he was an experienced camper and fended off young men harassing me. There was a time in Paris when we were in a crowd watching a street mime. Standing with my hands cupped behind my back, I felt a soft warmth that took a few moments to register: a man had parked his privates there. I snatched my hands away and nudged Malcolm to leave. *Pronto pronto.*

A few years later, I would have grabbed them and squeezed. Hard.

The late Fifties was a good time to travel: few tourists, fewer backpackers, and no crowded venues. Buying in street markets and eating frugally kept the cost for each of us on our nine-week odyssey by hired car through Holland, Belgium, Germany, Switzerland, Austria, Italy, France, Spain, Portugal, Spain and France again, including petrol, an occasional café meal or bottle of wine from a roadside cellar, down to £10 a week. Unthinkable today.

Reading about different countries took me so much further than I'd dreamt of, swaying in the branches of the flamboyant tree in Durban.

28

There was a reason for hurrying back in England: two of my Holland Park house mates and I had landed invitations to join the last-ever batch of young women from the Commonwealth to be 'presented' at Buckingham Palace, followed by a garden party. I bought an electric-blue dress, a cream hat, and a pale-yellow rose to tuck into my waistband. We were taught how to curtsey by the South African ambassador's wife. On the big day, we set off from our digs dressed up for the lark, wearing long white suede gloves.

A schoolfriend's brother, Derek, squired me to the palace in a swanky chauffeured Austen Princess borrowed from his father's firm. After flourishing my invitation at the palace gates, we swept into the inner courtyard where our partners were shown out to the garden while we were ushered up the grand staircase to the Throne Room, to hand our name cards to the courtier at the door.

Another courtier beckoned us to the thrones as our names were called out. Because the Queen wasn't well, we curtseyed to a benignly smiling Queen Mother and made a second curtsey to an obviously bored Prince Philip before sidling out sideways. Afterwards we heard that he had put his foot down on this outmoded display of colonial fawning, but I'm glad to have made it the last time.

Grand is how you feel descending that staircase, crossing the terrace and down the stone steps to the palace lawn, where you're swallowed in a crowd nibbling canapés and taking dainty sips of tea or bubbly. Winston Churchill shambled past as the crowd opened for him: an ancient tortoise with his head nodding low out of his morning coat, smiling an ancient party-lover's smile. Everyone clapped as he passed, still the hero.

My travels ended in an even grander finale. Hitch-hiking for a week through Scotland in late September with cousin Shirley, Malcolm's sister, we took a late-afternoon ferry to Skye and left our backpacks in the youth hostel to walk. The sound of bagpipes drew us to the sight of a kilted man playing outside his croft, a plaintive sound in keeping with the tranquil vista of loch and blue mountains.

As if summoned by the pipes, the darkening sky suddenly erupted in a shimmering canopy of brilliant light flecked with red, streaming from infinitely high. It was the aurora borealis, seldom seen so far south.

The radiance of that night remains as luminous in my memory as it was when the heavens danced to the music of bagpipes.

A few weeks later, Ron wrote to ask if I intended to come home, and if not, please to let him know. The best decision of my life was to abandon travel and supply teaching to hurry home on Trek Airways via Khartoum, heading for Lourenço Marques (now Maputo). As the plane touched down, I saw Ron hunched over the balcony rail of the airport building, having made an unexpected dash by car from Joburg. As romantic gestures go, it was a winner.

I had been missing him more and more, and 18 months is a long time.

While I'd met and partied with many people during my odyssey, I'd made it clear that my heart was in South Africa – and as such, was a safe proposition for blokes who were nervous about getting entangled.

To be closer to Ron, I took a secretarial job in Joburg and spent most of my spare time in his Hillbrow 'bachelor' flat. We were in the audience at the Wits Great Hall – the only venue where a 'mixed' audience was allowed then – when the first *King Kong* musical was memorably staged to audiences revelling in the township beat. Miriam Makeba's soaring rendition of *Back of the Moon* stays with me still. "Back of the Moon, boys, Back of the Moon, best shebeen in Joburg is Back of the Moon ..."

Within six months, local chemical construction projects went into a quiet phase. Ron decided to take leave of absence from his company to gain more experience by working in London, and flew off. There was no need to pop the question. We simply agreed that I'd go home to make arrangements for a wedding on 12 December 1959, in the Church of the Ascension over the road from St Anne's in Hilton.

Marrying young had never been my intention, but I had the good sense to snap up a special man before anyone else did. My luck was to have a father who didn't consider his daughter a mere girl on whom further education would be wasted when she landed a husband – the usual attitude of the time – and parents who respected my decisions.

Mostly. Mum was tweezer-lipped under her floral hat at the church and the cocktail wedding party in our garden afterwards because I'd chosen a trendy pattern flowing from my sternum for the dressmaker. People might think I was pregnant, she'd said. I compromised by having a well-fitted lower back finished off by a flaunting bow.

Calculating busybodies were proved wrong eleven months later.

Though I had made feeble attempts to write short stories in the London garret, a writing career was the last thing on my mind as we segued into the Sixties, heading for London again.

29

Our four-day honeymoon was spent with a planeload of passengers on a Trek Airways flight from Joburg back to London. Ron was working for an American chemical construction company, and I would return to supply teaching.

Those were the days when leisurely flights across Africa landed in strategic cities in the afternoons to overnight in hotels. There'd be time for an excursion, dinner, a good night's sleep and a full breakfast before taking off again. It was thanks to Trek Airways that I'd flown home via Khartoum at the confluence of the Blue and White Niles, a slow-moving mingling of pale and muddy browns, and encountered camels looking down their noses in the Omdurman market.

Our honeymoon plane flying north again was a Douglas DC-4 Skymaster that shook and juddered as it flew around thunderstorms. You could see the rivets jiggling in the wings. The sick bags in the seat pockets were there for a reason.

The first night's hotel at Entebbe had a wide-angle view of Lake Victoria and a giant mozzie net shielding us from battalions of mosquitoes. Next morning after breakfast we flew to Cairo and stayed at the Nile Hilton, where the comely lift attendants wore rearing-cobra headbands. For an extra fee, a tour bus took us past the Cairo Museum to view the pyramids and the Sphinx, then to a nightclub for a wobble-fest of belly dancing.

As we left the nightclub, a furtive *smous* pulled a bundle out of his inner pocket muttering, "Dirty postcards", which of course we bought. It folded down to a series of hilarious photos of Edwardian belles with bounteous bosoms, their interesting bits coyly veiled in wisps of gauze.

We should have kept it for posterity.

The Skymaster had four prop engines. After boarding at Cairo Airport next morning, one engine wouldn't start. We passengers sat goggle-eyed as the pilot and co-pilot climbed through a cockpit window onto the wing with spanners to try and fix it. No luck, they shrugged, returning to their seats.

"You all have to disembark now." The air hostess shooed us down the steps to stand at the edge of the tarmac as the plane took off on three engines, swooped about to start the fourth, and landed with all propellers whizzing, when we were ushered on board through exhaust fumes to fly to Malta.

I don't remember anyone protesting. In those days we trusted the intrepid pilots and nimble planes that hopped around Africa and to Europe, giving us access to affordable travel.

The flight over the desert was low enough for Padre Chutter, a chaplain who had served with the South African forces Up North, to point out the still-visible tank tracks in the desert around Tobruk, where he had been captured.

Our last night was in an agreeable Malta hotel. Next day we flew through the Alps with pine trees flicking past on both sides, bound for Luxembourg. A short flight from there in a bouncy Vickers Viscount landed us safely in London.

Marjorie was going on leave for three months, and had offered us the use of her flat opposite the hotel in Paddington while we found somewhere to live. By the time she returned, I had gone back to supply teaching, and we had secured a ground-floor flat in Kew Gardens near the tube station.

I was pregnant by then, and ignorant about the danger of over-exertion at three months. Our extreme labours cleaning every inch of

Marjorie's flat to prevent snarky comments about lazy South Africans resulted in a near miscarriage after we moved. Thus ended my teaching career.

A clanging ambulance ride from Kew to St Georges, the teaching hospital then at Hyde Park Corner, was my introduction to motherhood. To stop the bleeding and keep the baby, I spent a tedious month on my back in the gynae ward. It was summer and hot. London traffic honked all day outside the tall first-floor windows. I lay reading and trying to be a patient patient under the scrutiny of haughty specialists who swanned in twice a day to examine and pronounce on each patient, surrounded by scrums of junior doctors, the head sister and her team.

Modesty has no place in gynae wards, a useful preparation for future medical ordeals. I had always slept well, so wasn't given the thalidomide sleeping tablets then being dished out. That month's stay, two ambulance rides and the birth were courtesy the National Health. There were no pre-natal classes and labour went on all day, with no husbands allowed in the labour ward – the very idea!

However, there was laughing gas to inhale when I needed pain relief, and occasional junior doctors would drop in for a few whiffs at the gas mask too.

Our first daughter was born across the road from Buckingham Palace, but within hours developed a nasty boil from a lurking staphylococcus infection. A boil on a newborn's leg looks like Kilimanjaro, poor little thing. As more boils colonised both my breasts, I had to stop breastfeeding and we spent two more weeks there.

Discharged at last with antibiotics, Cow & Gate milk powder and bottles, back in Kew I'd lie in warm baths with her to soak our livid eruptions. We had a few visits from district nurses and went to the local clinic until the boils finally subsided.

One of the unsung advantages of feeding a baby – bottle or breast – is having time to read, so I got through more books than ever while feeding our babies.

Ron nobly schlepped our laundry to the launderette, furtively stuffing her soaked terry nappies into a washing machine as he tried to shield them from scrutiny by the watching row of seated women.

As soon as we were better, I walked her modest canvas pram (light years away from the sprung carriages of English babies) through Kew Gardens and into the tropical Palm House where the temperature and vegetation were so like Umzumbe. At weekends Ron and I strolled with the pram and our new SPCA mutt, Muggsy Spaniel, across Kew Bridge to the row of congenial pubs with outside benches along the river at Strand-on-the-Green.

Six months after her debut, we were due to set off for Scotland, where Ron had been posted to manage a construction site. He had bought an old car for £30: a 1935 Railton Straight 8 with a boxy ash body, eight cylinders, a l-o-n-g black bonnet, impressive headlights, leather seats and running boards.

She had to be cranked started by a strong arm, a process that went as follows: Husband opens bonnet. Primes engine with squirt of petrol from plastic bottle fished out from under driver's seat. Wife gets into driver's seat. Pulls out throttle. Makes sure gear is in neutral, brake on. Husband fits crank into hole. Wife poises foot over accelerator. Husband cranks. Nothing. Cranks again. Nothing. Re-primes engine with another squirt of petrol. Cranks again and again, sweating, until engine coughs.

Wife agitates accelerator. Engine catches. When throbbing to husband's satisfaction, he closes bonnet. Wife gets out and checks that baby's Moses basket is safely secured (no seat belts then). Gets into passenger seat. Husband inspects blisters on his cranking hand before stowing plastic bottle half full of petrol under driver's seat. Gets into driver's seat, releases brake – and we're off!

On a straight road the Railton went like the clappers. She was an elegant beast, though only did four miles to the gallon, unaffordable for regular driving. Once, Ron's cranking blisters flared up when he clapped his hand over the chimney of a paraffin lamp to stop it setting fire to the nappies it was drying. A throbbing red line started up his arm. The clinic doctor called an ambulance to rush him to a hospital with hand specialists where the virulent blood poisoning was vanquished. It was worse than the staphylococcus, and more dangerous.

By March we were ready to leave for Scotland and his on-site job at the Grangemouth Refinery near Edinburgh. Healed of infections and with high hopes, we headed north in the Railton with the baby in her basket on the back seat, bolstered by pillows, and Muggsy Spaniel in the well below her.

The radiator seized up before we had cleared the outskirts of London. Curses. We found a phone box, called a garage to fetch it, hailed a taxi to take us to a friend's share-house in Westminster and asked him to find a home for Muggsy. Then we took a train north, followed later by the fixed and railed Railton.

All costs were thankfully paid by the construction company.

The spacious flat rented for us was on the top floor of a grey stone house in Linlithgow, the beautiful loch town west of Edinburgh where Mary Queen of Scots was born. Because the construction work was nonstop, Ron worked every day during the nine months we lived there, including weekends … except one, when the Railton motored us and a varsity friend, Humph, to Loch Ness and back without a hitch.

My days were full attending to an increasingly active crawler and her needs. If it wasn't raining, I'd walk her in the pram round the town and loch, along a nearby canal, or up to the ruined castle. Between walks and nappy-changing, and on rainy days, I read a lot, wrote letters, made notes for stories and watched TV – a novelty, as it would only come to South Africa when that baby was a teenager. Sometimes I'd take a bus into Edinburgh to have coffee with the American construction wives, or walk her along Princes Street in the lee of the great castle on the crag.

We paid occasional evening visits to the construction families for feasts of barbecued spareribs, a new taste sensation. Our cranking routine was a hit as we prepared to drive away afterwards. One of the engineers boasted that he drove a Cadillac at home, "with everythin' in it but a douche bag".

In Linlithgow our landlady's daily, Mrs Thomson, came once a week to clean and iron, coo at the baby and entertain me with village gossip. Her husband Tam was a maltsman in the local whisky distillery, turning over the germinating barley on the malting floor until it was ready to shovel into a kiln for the next stage. On days when Mrs Thomson didn't come, I washed and mangled nappies using the landlady's old round swish-swish machine, hung them up and kept an eye out for rain, which meant another trek downstairs to haul them down and up to the flat to drape over the stair rails.

When a telegram arrived calling Ron home to work on, then manage, a construction job in Kitwe, we made plans at once to fly back to sunshine. Though we'd enjoyed Scotland, during those nine rainy months there were only three days when the sun shone all day.

We sold the Railton for £15, unable to afford shipping her home, or her prodigious thirst once there. What a beautiful beast she was.

30

Six months later we set off on a three-day marathon drive from Joburg to Kitwe, looking forward to a new challenge. This time, brighter facets of the dragonfly eye reflected a small red and white Austen A40 with a toddler sitting at the back in one of the flimsy hook-over car seats available then. It was February and sweaty-hot with no air conditioning as we headed north – and I was six months pregnant.

Highlight of the journey was a night in style at the Victoria Falls Hotel and a walk through the bush and teeming mist from the Falls in full spate, awe-inspiring up close. Before negotiating the steep descent to the Zambezi, border of what was then Northern Rhodesia, the car was sprayed for tsetse fly inside and out as we coughed and spluttered.

We had no inkling of the cramped mine house awaiting us, or the pungent reek of Kitwe's chimneys and industrial effluents. That ordeal didn't last long, as chemical engineers who'd work crazy hours were scarce. Soon we were moved to a more salubrious house opposite a park, staffed by a skilled Malawian, Philemon, who did the housework, cooking and ironing. Even the nappies had to be ironed for fear of putzi flies hatching and laying their larvae under delicate baby skin.

There was no time for writing in Kitwe besides occasional letters, though we met and socialised with other young parents. My kind mother-in-law Peggy journeyed up from Maritzburg to get to know her first grandchild and babysit during the new arrival. Taking advantage of the freedom to go out at night, we planned to see a movie with a new friend, Raymond, a South African engineer who worked for another firm on the construction site.

At the last minute, Ron couldn't come as he had to be on site for the plant's start-up, so Raymond bravely took me to the movie, hugely pregnant, with a due date several weeks ahead. Possibly spurred on by the Gothic drama of Hitchcock's version of *The Turn of the Screw*, our second daughter arrived in a hurry at Livingstone Hospital next morning. Ron just made it to the delivery room in time for her speedy arrival, the only birth he was able to attend. She shot out along the table into waiting rubber-gloved hands, to be greeted by her father's exclamation: "Just like a pig!"

He had witnessed dozens of piglet births while sharing the cost of breeding some Landrace pigs with a farmer friend, and for a spectator, all births must look the same. Partners don't get away so lightly these days.

Dr Spock saw me through her birth, many childhood ailments and her older sister's febrile convulsion that would have been terrifying without his advice. My tattered copy of that book had been passed on by the time our *laatlammetjie* fourth arrived, but I knew the ropes by then and will always be grateful for his reassuring presence in print.

We were a family of four when we drove south in December after the plant was up and running. There was time off to introduce the new arrival to the extended family, followed by a revitalising stay at Umzumbe before heading north again to the first home of our own: in Elandsdrift.

31

Inspired by rosy visions of life in the country and wanting our kids to grow up as farm children, we had bought a smallholding there before the Kitwe posting. It would be handy for Ron's construction work based in a steel pipe factory in Krugersdorp, and we had friends living a few miles away.

It was a good choice. Living in that singular community sparked my first serious writing, which continued for decades.

Elandsdrift is east of Muldersdrift and was a 20-minute drive north of Randburg. Lush farms and extensive estates along the Crocodile River were bordered by bare plots with a shack, a few gnarled peach trees and sometimes a derelict car on bricks. Crops ranged from extensive lucerne fields to mealie patches next to clusters of huts. Besides farmers and their workers, there were sheds of battery chickens, a pig farm, rented cottages, two trading stores, taxidermists, compost-makers, artists, potters, a diamond dealer, and some eccentric loners. In term time, kids ran along the roads to the farm school at Bultfontein.

On our ten-morgen (just over 20 acres) smallholding, the attractive-looking house was double storey, with a wood-shingle roof, semicircular rondavel ends, a large attic and a barn-sized outbuilding at the back. An expanse of bone-dry 'garden' and a slope of grassy veld ran down in front to a stream with a small dam, then a short way up the other side.

As first-time buyers, we were conned by the estate agent Robert van Tonder, later notorious as leader of the Afrikaner Weerstandsbeweging (AWB). We learnt after signing up for the property that he had lied about lowering the seller's price to £4,500, which we paid with the help of a bond. I marvel now at the blithe way we took on this big unfinished property that had surprises to come and consumed 15 years of hard work and bond payments – though it was a happy first home.

After moving in with minimal hand-me-down and sale-bought furniture, we spent our first few days prising huddles of palpitating frogs out of the empty sockets left for plugs near the floor, then sweeping them outside. In the kitchen, the crazy-paved slasto floors continued up the walls to waist height with ugly black grouting that stuck out and was sticky with cooking grease. It took a local builder nearly two weeks to chip off that slasto, re-plaster, tile and paint the wall.

With no Eskom yet, we dug into our savings to buy a paraffin fridge and a gas stove.

Next problem: the batteries that charged the feeble electricity system were powered by the diesel engine pumping up the borehole water. Each room in the house had a single globe dangling mid-ceiling, which meant that switching on more than three lights made them fade to dull orange.

The unfinished attic with dormer windows (plenty of room to expand, we had thought) was veiled in cobwebs and reached by a brick staircase that stopped halfway up, then continued with rickety wooden steps.

Besides the sparse pine trees along the back fence, there were a few syringas, a dying orchard, and a row of thriving Lombardy poplars with their roots in the French drain from the septic tank, which blocked up every few years. There are few more disgusting tasks than digging up a French drain clogged with roots and grey muck, precisely described by Mum's word for loathsome residue, 'goip'.

The outbuilding had a double garage and a storeroom without ceilings, and a three-room flatlet at the other end with a flush toilet and a shower. Soon we employed a small family who moved in: Solomon Molauzi, Angelina and two teenage daughters. He was a Malawian who had served with the British Army labour force in Mogadishu during the Second World War, showing it in the jaunty angle of his black beret. She was a proud Mosotho who rejected male dominance and was bigger than him, so it was a stormy relationship.

Living on a highveld smallholding is a constant challenge. Apart from drains that block up, you have to deal with rampaging fires roaring through long winter grass, ferocious storms and lightning, boreholes running dry, recalcitrant pumps, ticks, drought, floods, flaky neighbours, births, sickness and death.

Sometimes a cobra or rinkhals would rear up with a spread hood if disturbed near the house, or we'd find a night adder wriggling up a drain.

Our fluctuating livestock included bantams, hens, geese, ducks, three red setters, two disagreeable cats, and for a short while until the milking became too much trouble, a Jersey cow called Comfort. The poultry were known as The Feowls because the men in the grain store called their crushed mealies "feowl food".

At night we sometimes heard jackals howling and the distant roar of lions from the Lion Park over the hill behind Nana's store. Our days were punctuated by wild birds: red cardinals, yellow weavers, egrets, kingfishers, doves, shrikes, enraged kiewiets if you walked too close to their nests, and an occasional secretary bird stalking through the veld grass. Ibises gathered in a black-and-white flock round the pigsties of the farm across the valley. Owls lived in secret corners of the barn and sat silhouetted on the roof in the evenings before swooping down on faintly squeaking wings after field mice.

Swallows built mud nests in the open-ended garage each spring and taught their babies to fly off the telephone wires. In wet weather their nests sometimes slipped off the walls into poignant heaps of clay.

We had been there for several years when Solomon's left hand began to swell. A doctor who visited a nearby store diagnosed arthritis. When the hand didn't improve with medication, we took Solomon to our town doctor who came into the waiting room with an ashen face, saying he suspected leprosy.

It was like a bell tolling from the Middle Ages. By law, Solomon had to be taken at once by ambulance to Westfort near Pretoria, and the district surgeon came to take throat swabs from both families. All were negative because it is the one of the least infectious of diseases and well controlled by sulphonamides, which I learnt when I went to visit him and the hospital with its dedicated staff.

Uncontrolled leprosy absorbs bones as the nerves die, and causes skin lesions and ulcerating because sufferers don't feel pain from a burn or injury. I was shown around the hospital to meet fingerless men sewing with needles stuck between their stumps and healthy-looking children in school. There were still five white lepers in South Africa then, living in separate rooms next to their homes, isolated from their families and legally deprived of their right to vote.

The good news is that Westfort closed years ago as leprosy was effectively treated and declined in South Africa.

We were called to fetch Solomon after six weeks as the disease had been arrested, though he had to continue taking sulfa pills for life. But the third finger on one of his hands remained numb and irritated him while he worked. When he appeared one morning with a bloody bandage round its stump, he told us that he had cut it off and flushed it down the toilet.

32

Our third daughter arrived after lunch with friends in town and a dash to the Marymount. In Ron's judgement, a healthy baby included bright eyes and he never seemed disappointed that there were no boys, saying there was no need to "continue the family name".

He would have been bemused to know that they retained their Hobbs surname when they married, particularly in their working lives. He adored the grandchildren they gave us, though didn't live to meet the youngest.

As our daughters grew older, I made their dresses and some of mine – though why I spent hours sewing beats me now, as it was often frustrating and I didn't like handwork, apart from knitting while reading.

If I had that time again, we'd all be dressed by OK Bazaars, and I'd be writing with serious intent much earlier.

When the first three grew old enough to amuse themselves, I started writing in short spells at my desk. Soon the eldest started school at the Ursuline convent in Krugersdorp, dropped off by Ron on his way to work, and joined in time by her sisters.

Our weekly treat, apart from rare visits to the Velskoen Drive-in, was a drive to the Outspan Café in Muldersdrift for Sunday sweets and the *Sunday Times*. When they started school, the Outspan was where they were dropped off by the school Kombi; later the dropping-off place was extended to where the gravel road began.

Toiling in my study, absorbed in getting words on paper, took more and more time. I earned a bad reputation for being late after rattling along the gravel to fetch them, absorbed by what I had been writing. In a short story from that time, I wrote about the tedium of waiting for tardy parents:

> The sisters sat together on their school cases in the sparse shade
> of a thorn tree whose branches had been amputated on one side to
> make a tunnel for six humming telephone lines. Even the shade was
> hot. Dragon puffs of air swirled off the grit on the shoulders of the
> road whenever a car passed. Sometimes Libby played with stones
> while they waited, tossing them up to try and catch them on the
> back of her hand, six and more at a time as the cook's daughter did
> at home on the kitchen steps. Or she would range them in a span
> like oxen, with eight pairs of reddish-brown stones to pull a boulder
> wagon with yokes of curved twigs and traces of grass stalks stuck
> on with spit.

Communications in our valley were via wall-mounted party-line phones that had to be cranked to reach the tannie in the Muldersdrift post office exchange, whose chanted reply would be, "Mullies!" Our call sign was two short rings and two longs, and you could tell by a click if an eavesdropping neighbour on our circuit picked up to listen in.

Warm unpasteurised milk was delivered in one-gallon cans from friends with a few cows, and made delicious maas with a layer of cream on top. We made ginger beer with raisins that went up and down in the fermenting bottles, which sometimes blew up in the pantry.

Over the years there were more significant dramas. A light plane crashed into some trees on the way home from the school bus, and a father and young son died in the inferno. I hurried the children past when I saw a little fire-blackened arm sticking up from the wrecked cabin.

Lightning struck the trading store up the hill and burnt it down. Spectacular lightning storms are a regular feature of highveld summers, so children are well versed in not touching steel window handles, answering the phone or sheltering under trees if caught outside.

When a family that had fallen on hard times moved into the sparse rondavel next door, we felt sorry for them and sent across connections with water and electricity. The father repaid us by shooting and killing two of our red setters, wounding the third, because he'd found them going for his kids' rabbits. It was legal then to shoot marauding animals on farms, and however meek looking the setters were, three of them became a mob. After rushing the wounded one to the vet, our only recourse was to pull back both connections.

The family were soon gone, and Bunty and Bernard moved in. Red-haired Bunty offered to run a play school in our garden for the two pre-schoolers and some local farm kids. Bernard was an artist who painted watercolours and was particularly skilled at copying other artists' watercolours – notably a beautiful trout for Dad's birthday and a rearing Arab horse from a magazine cover for our wall.

We found our best-ever puppy in the newspaper smalls: a French bulldog cross we called Muggsy Bulldog – always known simply as Bulldog. She was lean and brindled with a white chest, ever-alert and friendly – too friendly, judging by her regular production of variegated offspring by itinerant fathers after coming on heat unnoticed.

The next drama happened while driving home on a rainy day in the little Austen with the kids. At a usually trickling causeway submerged under what looked like a few inches of water, I drove across and felt the car's wheels begin to slip sideways. In a reflex action, I stamped on the accelerator to surge out. We were lucky not to be washed off. It was an early warning not to underestimate the dangers of running water.

A later triumph was blowing the head off a rinkhals that had reared up in the garden and threatened our *laatlammetjie* two-and-a-half-year-old, who ran inside shouting, "Mummy! There's a soldier balancing on a piece of string." With the dogs barking hysterically, I realised at once what the 'soldier' must be, told her to sit down, rushed upstairs for the shotgun, made sure the dogs were clear, rammed in a cartridge and blew its head off. A rinkhals could spit poison in the dogs' eyes if they got too close.

We had to learn to deal with snakes over the years as they crept off the dry veld towards the house for water: mostly rinkhalses and night adders, and once a Mozambique spitting cobra. When a rocky outcrop was cleared by the gate leading down to the dam, Solomon dispatched the exiting serpents one by one and hung them along a tree branch, their tails still twitching with muscle spasms.

After the shotgun incident, my fame as a markswoman spread around the valley. Though people were allowed to have licensed guns on smallholdings, we had only used the shotgun to fire at clay pigeons – and once at a stray donkey chomping the daisies in a hard-won flower bed. It refused to be shooed off and stood with a defiant glare about ten metres away. Ron had fetched the shotgun to aim at its backside, hoping the sting of birdshot would send it off.

To his horror, it dropped dead. No one knew where it had wandered from. Burying a dead donkey with rigor mortis in hard-baked soil took Solomon several days, armed with a pickaxe and a dripping hose to ease the digging.

Life is challenging on smallholdings, and Solomon's Malawian savvy and muscle power were invaluable to inexperienced townies who had expected rural peace and quiet.

33

The good things about Elandsdrift were fresh air and living space.

When we could afford a carpenter, the attic became two big bed-rooms, one for us and one shared by the older three, with a small one in the middle for the fourth baby. Seven months pregnant, I hung wallpaper there, which is probably why she was born blue with the cord twice round her neck. She recovered within an hour, thanks to the skill of the natural-birth gynaecologist and the nuns at the Marymount.

A few years later, she and her friend Sillo spent a hilarious half hour flushing her stash of little broekies down the attic toilet until it blocked.

The plywood walls of the big bedrooms on either side were wallpa-pered, leaving triangular spaces under the eaves. After one Umzumbe visit, we came home to a plague of bedbugs in the big girls' bedroom that swarmed out to feast on them when they went to bed. Their bloodcurdling screams haunt me still. Getting rid of those bugs took four gas bombs and extensive spraying of the remaining critters that crept into the cracks under their wooden beds.

Attics have their secrets.

Sleeping up there gave our lives a different perspective. Once we woke to a hot-air balloon parping outside our dormer window. Grass fires made a sound like running water, and when we heard the liquid crackling at night and saw orange light dancing on the walls, everyone turned out with hoses and wet hessian sacks nailed to broom handles to keep the fire away from the buildings. For the next week walking on the black tufts in the veld crunched under our ashy shoes until green shoots came up and the veld grew again to a swathe of spring green.

No TV and no friends nearby meant that the girls became keen readers, sometimes up the mulberry tree – is there a special magic to reading in trees? – and created their own games. Besides their birthday parties, for some years we held an annual pre-Christmas feast for town friends with singing and dancing and kids running about in the dark.

Eldest daughter fell in love with horses at an early age, voraciously reading horse books, and taking riding lessons on a naughty white pony called Mgundwane. One day (probably after some nagging) I foolishly bought two horses at a farm auction, which Solomon led home. They turned out to be impossible to catch, let alone ride. We called the hairy grey gelding Army Blanket and Solomon named the palomino mare Viole(n)t. She then surprised us with a red chestnut foal we called Rufus.

By now, Ron had also caught the horse bug. After selling on the first three unrideables, he bought a succession of more suitable horses. Now there were two pairs of saddles and bridles in the storeroom and father and daughter went riding together, exploring the valley and koppies. Ron must have had a genetic predisposition to riding, as one of his grandfathers had been a saddler sergeant in the Boer War, having come from an English family of saddle-makers and horse owners.

The rest of us made plucky attempts, but since there are no brakes on horses, preferred to stay on terra firma. We read in one of our growing numbers of horse books that a Bishop of Cork had called them "foolish farting creatures".

Father and daughter had many long rides together over our years in Elandsdrift. Their horses ranged, two at a time, from a greedy youngster called Sugar Plum Fairy (who'd throw off her rider and rush back to the stable for her food, so had to go), to a steady Basotho pony, Robbie, to calm Misty to fiery Sergeant and an elegant ex-racehorse, Sabre, who would follow you around like a puppy.

The current pair of horses were stabled together in the converted garage where our bantam chickens roamed, pecking up the dropped oats. Sometimes a chicken got trampled on, but after recovering, gamely limped about on crooked legs.

Second daughter dissected the Mozambique spitting cobra which disgorged eggs, then left it near an ant-heap where it was soon a curve of delicate bones in her 'museum'. This also had a Stone Age hand axe commandeered from Ron, who had picked it out of a pile of stones – hardly a surprise, as we weren't far from Sterkfontein Caves. She has been fascinated by archaeology and middens ever since.

Third daughter, quiet and watchful, bided her time in the general family racket and nurtured Muggsy's variegated puppies in their whelping box. One of them clearly had Weimaraner ancestry, and we kept two that were just like her, before having her spayed for relief from unseen nocturnal suitors on the prowl.

Youngest daughter directed visiting friends in short plays she wrote, costumed from the dressing-up box, before growing up to study Drama at university. One morning when asked why she'd gone out early into the dewy garden, she said, "I'm just admiring the world."

We forget the fresh delights of being young and impressionable.

Apart from occasional visits to and from friends and to the drive-in, we'd pay rare visits to one of the few pasta or burger places in town. A special highlight was venturing into the depths of Sterkfontein Caves with our headlamp lights glancing off dripping stalactites and eerie lagoons of black water.

Parents try to do their best, not always successfully. In the early Seventies, we were inspired by the nutrition guru Adelle Davis and her book *Let's Get Well* to launch into a regime of healthy eating. The daughters have hilarious memories of the home-made bread which I taught our housekeeper Angelina to bake. It was made with stone-ground flour and fresh yeast, delicious when warm from the oven and loaded with cheese and pickles or slathered with butter and jam. The problem lay in their school sandwiches: dense cold doorstops which – we learnt much later – they either swapped for white-bread sandwiches or put in the Poor Box at the convent.

They did moan (a lot) about Adelle's Tiger's Milk, which we made to fortify their breakfasts. It was an admittedly disgusting mixture of fresh milk, powdered milk, brewer's yeast, wheatgerm, banana and honey that came out of the blender thick and bubbly like warm sick. It would keep them fit and strong, we warbled, watching as they feigned taking agonised sips. After we'd left the room, they told us (again later) that they'd thrown the rest onto the roots of two rose bushes outside the windows.

We should have realised that those bushes grew as high as the gutters and flowered with such abundance because they were so well nourished.

With Solomon's help, we finished and fenced a half-built swimming pool which became an important part of their childhood in summer, playing 'Marco Polo' and swimming like happy fishes. Ron had spent much of his childhood at the Maritzburg swimming baths, and he taught them the correct swimming strokes. They remember eating tinned peaches lying tummy-down on the hot slasto pool surround or stretched on towels in the shade of the syringa – the worst possible pool-side tree. First their flowers dropped in the water, then their leaves, and last their dry berries that invariably clogged the Kreepy Krauly.

Our next project was a clay tennis court in a former orchard, using a truckload of ant-heaps. Uncle Jake's dumpy level and measuring pole helped us measure a level surface with six-inch nails hammered by Solomon into the flattened ant-heaps. A stamper and roller bought at a farm sale smoothed it off. Having saved up for poles, net and boundary fencing, we played with local friends on a fine gravel court with nailed-on plastic lines as our kids disappeared to play their own games.

Their favourites were Cops and Robbers, *Skop die Blik* and an invented game they called Judge, in which sentenced malefactors were jailed for a few minutes in the dark cool-room.

Once while we were hunched over the dining table with friends trying to teach us bridge, four of our offspring were perched on the high beams above the stable in the outbuilding, taking turns with a pellet gun to shoot at the rats in the straw below. One ricocheted shot just missed third daughter's eye. Naturally we weren't told about it until she confessed the incident years later, after the instigator had become an advocate who helped to admit her as an attorney to the High Court.

Driving home from delivering a manuscript to town late one holiday morning, worried about what they'd been up to in my absence, I found them waving from the peak of the high roof. They had climbed out a dormer window from the attic onto the flat roof above the kitchen and crawled up the wood shingles, which were treated every five years with old engine oil from the garage to prevent them curling up in the heat.

Living out there gave them an untrammelled (if sometimes grubby) early life during which they learnt to be self-reliant. My occasional working mother's guilt was a fraction of the mothers' guilt they suffered when they grew up and started work in a busier, more demanding urban world.

Elandsdrift was a simple life with homely (if sometimes risky) pursuits. I can't remember who first joked about calling it Hobbs Hall, but as we carried on the name to subsequent houses, it became in time Hobbs Hall I.

Twice a year we took the long road to Umzumbe and the beach.

34

In the mid-Sixties, I was asked to be manager of the Lebogang farm school in nearby Bultfontein. They needed a white person's signature for official documents, and a mailing address to receive the monthly cheques for five teachers, which I collected with the post in our Muldersdrift postbox.

The farm school had been started by Quakers in 1940 and run by them until they were forced out in 1955 by Bantu Education. The children came from poorly paid farm workers' families. When winter came that year, I wrote to *The Star* asking for donations of warm clothing, which resulted in several bakkie loads arriving from Operation Snowball.

The Lebogang headmaster, Mr R.K. Phambane, would come to fetch the monthly cheques for his teachers and we'd chat over tea. His accounts of their struggles in crowded classrooms were a stimulus to more action. I suggested asking SAVS, a voluntary students' organisation at Wits University, to fund and build another classroom during their Christmas vac, and he was delighted.

The students who came to camp there enjoyed the work and the camaraderie, and the new classroom was soon finished. In January the enlarged school opened with 390 children, some walking and running many kilometres to get there.

My well-meant meddling led to its demise. In December 1970 a terse letter from the Bantu Education office in Krugersdorp ordered that it be closed, as there had been a petition from nearby smallholders.

When I phoned them to protest, a spokesman said it was government policy not to let farm schools accommodate more than 100 children.

Actual quote: "If the schools get too big there is a danger of them becoming black spots. It is a sign that there is too much concentration of the population there."

The petitioners complained that the kids running to school were a hazard on the roads and crept through their fences along the way to steal peaches.

I contacted our local Member of the Provincial Council and we went in a delegation to Pretoria to beg Piet Koornhof, then Minister of Education, to keep it open. With his familiar avuncular smile, Koornhof said that the new classroom had attracted too many children, the neighbours were complaining, and he had to listen to his voters. *Wragtig*. But as a concession, he would allow the school to stay open until June so the learners and teachers would have time to find other schools.

It was a cruel blow. Other 'Bantu' schools were too far away to walk to, though some kids were squeezed into a school on a nearby farm that belonged to Jim Bailey, the founder of *Drum* magazine. Mr Phambane was relocated to Soweto. I still have the sad letter he wrote from the Salvation Army Hostel thanking me for my kind attempts to help the school.

Was it kind to interfere in a process that enabled access to learning for deprived children? Looking back, it's a depressing reminder that good intentions can have bad consequences.

35

Unlike today's moveable feast of work spaces, in the Sixties and Seventies working from home wasn't considered actual work. This was the prevailing mindset when women started families in our early twenties while the man of the house went nobly off to earn the bread.

There were advantages to this scenario: we didn't struggle to get pregnant, took babies in our ignorant stride, matured fast and managed on one salary, saving up for Big Things. With a well-employed husband and domestic help during the week, I could write from home earning the piddling amount freelancing paid then, which could never have supported a family.

The disadvantages were that less busy women felt free to drop in for coffee and a chat or, since I was working from home, ask me to fetch their kids with mine if they had important meetings or appointments. Employed people confined to formal working hours didn't consider my flexible hours to be anything like their hard labour.

At a business dinner in the Seventies, a captain of industry leant towards me and said, "I hear you're a writer? It must be nice to earn some pin money."

Pin money! My *Brewer's Dictionary of Phrase and Fable* defines it as, "A woman's allowance of money for her own personal expenditure … Pins were a great expense, and in 14th and 15th century wills there are often special bequests for the express purpose of buying pins."

Condescension from bosses came with wives' territory then.

Bosses are sometimes guilty of the #MeToo moments that continue to happen all too often to women. Only recently have we been speaking out about the persistent gropers and touchy-feely men living in the past who still think it's okay to pat or fondle bottoms.

My first moment, as already mentioned, was the man who parked his privates into my hands cupped behind my lower back in a Paris crowd. As a naive twenty-one-year-old, I was too embarrassed to do more than snatch my hands away and leave.

The second time happened in 1970 in Rome where I'd met Mum and David for a brief onward sortie to England and Norway. We were in the Vatican Museum admiring the sculpture of Laocoön and his sons writhing in the grasp of serpents when a man came up behind me and thrust his hand between my legs under my crotch. For visiting the holy of holies I'd worn the latest fashion, a lime-green pantsuit that stood out like algae in a pond of water lilies. This time I turned round yelling and clocked him with my shoulder bag. I had blanked out the memory until David reminded me.

Superseding these and other minor invasions, like the time I was taken for a prostitute walking down a deserted street on a foggy London evening and the inevitable frottage in crowded Tube trains, was a nasty incident on a South African train that I still find hard to believe.

It was long ago in the July holidays when trains were considered safe. Ron was away on business and I was travelling by train to Durban with four children to join my family in Umzumbe. Our older two must have been five and three, and we had a six-year-old friend with us. Our third daughter was still a baby.

As we pulled out of Germiston, I ordered and paid for a coffee and cool drinks for the kids from the chief steward. They came on a tray carried by a young steward. I was sitting down when he entered, with the baby in her basket next to me. The older three were scrambling between the top bunks, excited about sleeping on a train. Underneath the tray, the steward's fly was open, and his naked penis stood erect, level with my eyes.

I decided not to make a fuss in case the children saw it. So I took the tray and after hesitating, he turned away and left. I'm still not sure whether he expected a shock-horror reaction, or if wanking to threaten women passengers gave him a buzz. After settling the kids down, I spent a sleepless night worrying what to do. Would I be believed? By morning, I'd decided to report him so he didn't threaten other women or young girls like mine.

In the morning I called and told the chief steward, who was horrified and gasped, "But he's a student!" with the reverence of a worker for academia.

I needn't have worried. He brought the young steward for me to identify, then hustled him away. Dad met us on Durban Station and was equally horrified when I confided what had happened. The kids hadn't noticed anything.

That night I had such a terrifying pain on top of my head that I thought it could be an aneurysm or a stroke. Dad rushed me to Port Shepstone Hospital. After the emergency doctor had checked me and heard the story, he said it was probably tension, injected a muscle relaxant and suggested physiotherapy. By the time we got back to the cottage, the pain had gone.

Since then, even dancing with a large friend who held me too close to a suspiciously hard banana under his fly has felt like – well, small bananas set against the atrocities of humiliation and rape told by so many women. They range from war victims to desperate refugees, to employees too scared to report superiors because they need their jobs, to actors of both sexes who have been preyed on for decades by the jackals of the film and theatre worlds.

It makes me proud that many women are standing up to the

penises now, but immensely troubled that the vast majority are help-less against rampant men and domineering patriarchy. What can we do for our violated sisters beyond acknowledging that they are worse off than we are, and demanding legal action?

My generation hit our forties with older children leaving the nest and a good idea of what we wanted to do with the rest of our lives. A friend with a science degree was accepted into medical school and became a GP who was still working well into her seventies. Others went back to university, became lawyers or lecturers, returned to teaching, started businesses, or worked for charities.

After the home-centred years, our motivation was huge. So is our current schadenfreude at the sight of career mothers in their forties and fifties panting after their toddlers.

School days gave me more time to think and write, and working at home fitted in well with the family. Rattling along the gravel road to fetch them from the school Kombi in the afternoons, I'd mull over ideas for stories based on the lives of the people who lived around us.

My reputation for being late to fetch them grew – unjustly, I felt. But explaining that I had lost track of time as I worked on a story didn't impress hungry schoolkids who had been toiling at their desks for *hours*.

36

Some years later, a friend from university days, Marilyn Hattingh, moved with her young twins to Jim Bailey's farm to tutor the older Bailey kids. We'd visit each other and talk while her twins played with our youngest. Having studied law, she'd done some teaching and spent several years writing for and editing magazines. Soon she was appointed editor of *Darling*, a women's magazine, and moved to Durban to work at the Republican Press HQ in Mobeni.

With the savvy of the quintessential editor she became, she identified friends she believed could produce copy for *Darling*, and asked them to write for her. I was cajoled to write a column.

"What sort of column?" I bleated.

"Just write a few and I'll tell you which I like. About 1,500 words."

Jawellnofine. Should I write something romantic, critical or funny?

Dreaming up ideas for that column was my start in freelance journalism, which expanded over 20 then 30 years to umpteen articles and short stories, 22 editions of 12 books and a career working from home – though I could never have supported myself, let alone a family, on my earnings.

From the four initial pieces I sent her, Marilyn chose the one ostensibly told by an ex-stripper whose act included swinging shongololos – inspired by the scandalous local stripper Glenda Kemp and her python Oupa. *When I Danced the Last Tango* was my first attempt at satire in the South African English vernacular, including squiff spelling. (It was renamed *Larst Tangoe in Parys* in the subsequent collection of *Blossom* columns.)

A single comment had set me off: hearing a mother say to a child who had just won a competition, "Hang, but you clever, hey?"

Masquerading as a 'Joburg working chick from Bez Valley', Blossom Broadbeam grew out of that first column in March 1973 and struck an immediate a chord with *Darling* readers. Her family – Mom and Dad, Ouma, Auntie Vilma and My Boet, plus assorted boyfriends, bosses and her pellies Charmaine and Lorna – starred fortnightly for the next seven years on the *Darling* back page, and later in *Femina* after *Darling* closed and Marilyn moved on to initiate the upmarket *Style* magazine.

Journalism couldn't be studied then. People with a good grasp of language wrote after studying various publications to suss out what readers preferred. Blossom's lingo came from words and phrases heard in the streets during occasional forays to Randburg and Krugersdorp, at farm sales and from the chit-chat of teenagers. I remained anonymous as her creator.

She soon had fans all over the country, including Dr Jean Branford of Rhodes University, author of Oxford University Press's *A Dictionary of South African English*. A collection of those columns titled *Darling Blossom*, illustrated as usual with cartoons by Leo Kritzinger, was my first book, published in 1979. Jean wrote in the foreword:

When a friend sent me a column of Blossom's in 1974 not only did I laugh until I cried, but I felt all the excitement of Keats's

watcher of the skies
When a new planet swims into his ken;
Or like stout Cortez when with eagle eyes
He star'd at the Pacific...

for the first time. Here was what I, as a student of 'South African English' had been waiting for — a writer who 'held up the mirror to nature' and truthfully recorded the colloquial language of young and not so young South Africans ...

I have met her fans in many walks of life and among types as wildly divergent as a burly Cambridge PhD in water-engineering, a long-haired and bearded classical musician, a little lady behind the counter of a country junk shop and a solemn-eyed drama student who wanted to 'do Blossom' but her tutor didn't think her accent up to it!

To read Blossom is to love her — except perhaps in the case of those whom her satirical cap may fit uncomfortably tightly — and the appearance of this volume of *Darling Blossom* will be, I am sure, as great a delight to her chommies and pellie blues everywhere as it is to me.

She writes with a light but sure touch and with endless inventiveness and humour, but however much she makes fun of her characters her wit is never cruel nor her satire harsh. Furthermore, her faculty for acute linguistic observation never fails her and she uses a consistent, carefully formulated spelling system calculated to reflect without grossness many characteristics of South African English pronunciation. Also her vocabulary and grammar faithfully render much of what one hears around one every day in many places.

Ouma, Auntie Vilma, my Mom and Dad and my boet, not to mention the Bez Valley crowd, Bok-Bok McGuire, Lorna, Frik, Dumbo and Charmaine-and-them should eventually become as real to South Africans as the Gileses are to the British ... Within the short space of four years, with the limitations of a fortnightly appearance in a magazine primarily for women, Blossom and her circle have endeared themselves to thousands to whom they are pure joy ...

Safe my mate and more power to yore trusty ballpoint.

Thanks to Jean, the Bez Valley chick who couldn't spell for toffee apples was immortalised in the second edition of *The Oxford English Dictionary* in 1986. The entry under 'Ag' read:

> 1975 *Darling* (S Afr.) 'Ag, shame,' she babbles on, 'you should of stayed by me, Bloss!'

Other words from *Darling Blossom* and a later novel are also referenced in the OED, including 'bioscope', 'monkey's wedding', 'mompara' and 'rugger-bugger'.

Writing in Blossom's voice was an exploration of our lively *mengsel* of languages. I'd grown up with a Dad who revelled in puns and limericks, which led naturally to writing doggerel and satire for school magazines, though I often grow fond of characters I intend to parody. Humour has been a consistent element of my writing ever since.

Blossom was brought alive in the Sandown Hall in early August 1983 in a one-woman show *Darling Blossom*, starring actress Elma Potgieter and directed by Schalk Jakobsz. Reviews were mixed. Critics enjoyed the character, but not her delivery. Raeford Daniel wrote:

> Blossom belongs as irrevocably as biltong, braaivleis and Dr Danie Craven ... We cannot but respond with warmth to her effervescent enthusiasm ... [despite] the breakneck speed at which her words come tumbling out and her often shrill delivery.

She didn't last long on stage in upmarket Sandton.

The places Blossom inhabited as a white chick from Bez Valley who jolled in Hillbrow were transformed as our country loosened the stranglehold of apartheid, and her langwidge is way out of date now. But for those who *smaaked* the Seffrican of the Seventies, she was an icon. At my book launches readers sometimes mention her, quoting favourite columns like *Sweet Soos Sauer Street* or *Kêrel by Candlelight*, and reminiscing about her family and mishaps.

To my surprise, I still receive occasional requests for the book, of which only 2,000 were published. Rare copies on internet sites can fetch up to R1,000. In 1979 the cost was R2.95. It's a neat example of the value of first editions – especially only editions.

Ag shame, all past history now. But I'm pleased to have written the first regular column in South African English which continues to thrive and develop as living languages should, joyously incorporating words from other Mzansi languages as we communicate between cultures.

"Talk about integration, hey?" Blossom would have said.

My other minor claim to fame is having named the Midlands Meander. It was conceived and started in 1985 by my brother David and a group of friends working as potters, weavers, painters and craftspeople in their studio homes in the Natal Midlands. He phoned from his pottery in the old wood-and-iron mill at Caversham, asking me to think of a name they could call their proposed art and craft route. After some thought, I had two suggestions.

They chose Midlands Meander, which became a flourishing component of KwaZulu-Natal tourism, creating employment in Midlands enterprises that offer diversions for travellers and weekenders. The idea of visiting country crafters in their home studios inspired other art and craft routes, including the Crocodile River Ramble where our potter friend Tim Morris lived with his family and worked in his studio. David's experience of working with Tim during a long stay with us had led to his studying Fine Arts, specialising in Ceramics at university with Michelle, whom he married. Driving past Midlands Meander signs on the N3 gives me a tremendous kick and an ever-deeper understanding of the power of words – even just two.

In a sad postscript, the 135-year-old corrugated-iron Caversham mill and its yellowwood beams and giant water wheel were washed away by flooding after torrential rain during a prolonged storm at the end of September 1987. Trees swept downstream by the raging Lions River jammed the low-level bridge nearby, flooding its banks.

Their stone-built home stood fast with water swirling through its top floor and gushing out the downstairs windows as they took shelter up the road. After he and the family left Caversham for a decade in England, it changed hands and remains an attraction on the Midlands Meander, now a country restaurant with cottage accommodation. And views of the river purling down a waterfall from the bridge, peaceful as a lamb, overlooked by the empty site where the mill once stood.

Kwa-Zulu Natal has become notorious for raging floods that wash its fertile red-brown topsoil into the sea, scouring out valleys, sweeping away homes and schools and roads, clinics, sewerage and infrastructure. The Western Cape has followed suit. Climate change is upon us.

37

After 15 Elandsdrift years of gravel roads, veld fires and smallholding dramas, Lanseria Airport was established too close for peace and a new highway was planned that would cut across our property – though it was never built. Aghast at the onslaught of progress, we sold in 1978 and moved to town.

Urban house prices having plummeted, we could afford to buy in upper Parkview. Double-storey Hobbs Hall II was built against the rocky cliff where steep flights of public steps lead up between thickets of bush to Westcliff. Recent owners had added an ultra-modern living room jutting out one side, and a sheltered pool between the house and the cliff.

We created another ant-heap tennis court, slightly shorter than usual to fit into the front lawn, flanked by a rockery, which is my favourite way of creating an instant garden with succulents, aloes and rambling nasturtiums.

By then the older girls were busy teenagers in high school, heading for different universities.

My freelance work grew with longer working hours and quicker access to the Republican Press offices in End Street to drop off copy. I could attend launches and meet the editors of *Scope, Farmer's Weekly, Garden and Home, Living & Loving* and *Bona*. Editors were always looking for new ideas and stories, and the offices were fertile ground for new assignments.

RP's best-selling *foto-romans* books were black-and-white photo comics that ranged from *skop, skiet en donner* to cowboy stories, medical dramas and romances – early versions of graphic novels.

My sole contribution to *foto-romans* was a self-protection issue detailing how a woman could defend herself if attacked while alone. One of the props was a broom handle. What the advice didn't say was that a male attacker was usually stronger and meaner, and could grab the broom handle away.

The challenges of freelancing included how to vary writing for different readers. I wrote mainly for South African magazines and newspapers: short stories, book reviews, satire and think-pieces. Sometimes I'd use an alternative name in the byline, a common practice then. Editors who were short of copy would request fillers to close gaps – or do it themselves.

When I wrote what I thought was a good enough short story, I sent it to *Contrast* or another literary publication under my own name. Most were rejected, but thanks to my friend Jane in London who was working for a publisher, some were published in the UK – including two in *Argosy*, the fabled English short story monthly that expired in 1974.

Living in the suburbs also meant that I was able to tackle articles with personal interviews or broader research. If you had a decent camera, you could illustrate your own work. For years I used the Kodak Retina I'd bought in Germany for my twenty-first birthday, which took excellent transparencies. Later I added an old-fashioned Mamiya Super Press bought from a professional RP photographer, which took spectacular 6mm x 9mm transparencies of interiors with a wide-angle lens, and portraits with a standard lens. Since it was heavy and old, it had to be schlepped around with a tripod and a separate light meter to decor makeovers in Berea, Soweto and later Cape Town.

Typescripts and transparencies were submitted by hand then,

before the advent of the internet, though some of today's journalists write and illustrate articles with smartphones that transmit high-quality digital images in a flash.

Despite the convenience of living closer to town, there was a major drawback to living in Parkview: no room for a horse. With our eldest daughter by then away at university, Ron spent his Sunday mornings riding a hired steed alone on the mine dumps, Joburg's toxic desert landscape. Within two years we had moved again, to a gabled bungalow on three acres in Bryanston where the houses thinned towards Witkoppen, and a horse could crop the veld.

Hobbs Hall III's drawback was too few bedrooms, so we added a two-bedroomed cottage with interleading facilities for the remaining teenagers – the second of whom nobly slept in the pantry until it was ready, as her sister was writing Matric.

Happy to be able to ride his own horse again, Ron bought an Arab gelding he called Hamzah, and volunteered as a mounted River Ranger. This meant patrolling the Braamfontein Spruit on a weekend roster, dashing in khakis with green shoulder tabs, a ranger's hat, a whistle on a lanyard and a walkie-talkie. To join him sometimes, I bought a mountain bike and rode on the uneven path running beside the river. Before long, he also bought a bike and soon we were cycling more seriously in our mid-fifties.

Adding as needed, Hobbs Hall III was the home we lived in longest, for the next 20 years. We glassed in the stoep between the gables, lengthened the old pool at the bottom of the garden to a salt-water lap pool with a rockfall of trickling water, a koi pond and brick paving supplemented by railway sleepers, which only cost R1 each if fetched from the depot. At the far end, a thatched lapa with a round wooden hot tub sheltered by woven reed mats from Kenya completed the pool area, and was a respite after working days.

The movable hot tub was a place to chat about our days after a bike ride or just lie back and think. I had some of my best ideas in the hot tub, massaged by cascades of warm bubbles which extended lines of thought in unexpected ways.

A shady pin oak on what passed for a lawn sheltered meals with family and friends, including breakfasts cooked by Ron and any boyfriends present on a meter-long steel skillet heated by two gas rings, as we women sat *skindering*.

Our daughters learnt to drive in a grandpa's old car, bouncing over tussocks in the veld. Two of them married in the Eighties with homely receptions in a lawn marquee, followed by the third sister's some years later. The first grandkids learnt to swim off the pool's wide shallow step, jumped off the rocks at the slightly deeper end, ventured into the nearby bamboo jungle, and joined us in the hot tub.

Those were good days before our lives darkened.

38

By the Seventies Ron was managing two pipe companies, one in Krugersdorp and one in Germiston, and the newly constructed ring road gave him easier access to both, though it meant a lot of driving.

As did a road trip in 1982 visiting far-flung pipe factories in De Aar, Port Elizabeth and Cape Town. Since we had both gone on holiday in steam trains as kids, a special attraction was the railway junction at De Aar, the navel of our country's rail network, where steam locomotives were still working on the Kimberley line.

It took a long time to get there from the N1, with the road like a tarmac ruler narrowing to the horizon, laid across land so arid that even the scrubby grey *bankrot* bushes battled to survive. The only signs of life were knots of dusty sheep, heads bowed in the heat, until the small Karoo town emerged under its pepper trees, hot and silent in the afternoon, and we could cool down under fans in the country hotel.

Next day while Ron visited the factory, I showed my press credentials and was taken to see the clanging workshops where aging locomotives were being overhauled to prolong their working life. The foreman Mr Etzebeth brought out the visitors' book, signed by steam buffs from around the world who came to see the engines being upgraded and take photographs of steam in action.

A mechanic took me round the forlorn resting place of 150 decommissioned locomotives in the shunting yard, naming them as we went. Particular models earmarked for preservation had been brought to De Aar, stripped of reusable parts and lined up on rail spurs, coupled together in a last handclasp.

Except for the soft moan of wind blowing through jagged windows, the curving corridors between rows of old locomotives were silent. Weeds grew among the rails. Tumbleweeds had piled up against iron wheels and cowcatchers. In the cabs, the black mouths of furnaces gaped where red-hot fires once roared, the great workhorse pistons they had driven stilled, the metal drivers' seats empty.

Like the pair of old shoes I saw abandoned on a carriage platform, the old steam giants had outlived their useful lives.

It was the melancholy end of an era – and a photographer's dream. What a perfect setting it would have made for a thriller. Stealthy footsteps crunching on moonlit gravel. Fingers scrabbling against flaking steel. Crouching shadows flitting across silhouettes of cabs, boilers and top-hat chimneys ...

In my later teenage novel *Video Dreams*, I created a scene where the main character, rebellious Sylvie, and her bank-robber boyfriend are in De Aar looking for a place to hide, and find the old steamers:

It was eerie walking between those huge iron wheels with weeds growing up through them and broken windows crunching on the gravel under our boots. The coupling hoses at the front and back of each unit looked like drooping grey trunks, as though it was a place where elephants go to die.

With platteland hospitality we were invited for a braai that night, and regaled with chat about traction, live steam and the old days on the footplate.

Everything in De Aar centred on the railways. Residents were knowledgeable about the massive locomotives that chuntered back and forth in the shunting yards, or stood waiting for refitting outside the machine shops.

As we enjoyed succulent Karoo lamb chops and boerewors, they spoke of the steam giants as departed old friends. The dry Karoo climate was a good place to stage them, they said. The De Aar depot included special railway carriages intended for a future museum, and there were more locomotives and carriages mothballed at Beaufort West and Touws River.

But in 1997 the final Trans-Karoo steam train pulled into De Aar, and all too soon every one of those magnificent machines had gone. Apart from the models bought by preservation groups of steam enthusiasts, the rest of the mothballed locomotives were sold as scrap iron. Mostly to China.

There is some good news, however. In 1985 entrepreneur Rohan Vos decided to start a vintage train business. His first few purchases grew to a small fleet of trains running regular journeys between the main depots in Pretoria and Cape Town, with occasional longer excursions to Dar-es-Salaam or Windhoek. All are popular with tourists, though expensive for locals.

In 2009 I was invited to join a complimentary family group on a Cape Town to Pretoria journey, and hugely enjoyed reliving childhood train journeys in undreamt-of style. Given a bubbly send-off in a classy suite of rooms at Cape Town station, we were soon trundling through lush valleys and later the Karoo.

After steaming out of Cape Town, for logistical reasons our leisurely progress to Pretoria was drawn by diesel engines. Our journey also included stops for excursions in Matjiesfontein and Kimberley.

The train had a lounge in the last carriage with a bar and an open observation deck for watching the world chug by. Gourmet meals were served in a vintage dining coach with a squadron of Cape wines to savour, and passengers were asked to dress for dinner, which meant elegant evening meals. Rocking to sleep on a winter's night was like old times as we clickety-clicked on, shunted now and then into side spurs to let mainline trains through.

The journey was magnificent. Think the Orient Express with African hospitality dispensed by a skilled staff who were passionate about steam. The grand finale was pulling into Capital Park station in Pretoria wreathed in steam again, to see a shed of immaculate puffing billies with shining brass trimmings being fettled for their next journeys.

It was another photographer's dream, with a pleased old engine driver leaning an elbow out of our cab, his face seamed by long years of service.

In such a way the glamour of train travel lives on around the world for steam aficionados who can afford the cost of timeless luxury. All that's missing is Hercule Poirot twirling his moustache.

A sad aspect of our journey was being confronted, even then, by the tragic deterioration of the rail network. Barbed wire surrounded trashed ticket offices and waiting rooms where even the corrugated iron roofs had been stolen.

Shame on Transnet, whose lack of security has meant that looters have stolen our railway heritage and commuters' off-road transport, rail by rail, sleeper by sleeper, and station by station.

In De Aar the ghosts of the old railway elephants trumpet in vain.

39

My deeper understanding of our country's bitter struggles began when I started working on a new magazine for black women.

Republican Press's market leader, *Bona*, is still published monthly in four languages: isiZulu, isiXhosa, English and Afrikaans. In the mid-Seventies, the owners planned a women's supplement, *Thandi*, which would start as an insert in *Bona*. I was offered the job of Features Editor.

Accepting the challenge would be a radical shift from the magazines I had worked on, going way beyond my white suburban boundaries. While I felt confident about writing for my usual readers, the needs and aspirations of women of colour were, to quote L. P. Hartley about the past, a foreign country. By the Nineties I wouldn't have accepted such a possibly contentious assignment. But Republican Press was a gung-ho organisation run according to the instincts of the Hyman magazine moguls, and if they thought I was up to it, I agreed to try.

Planning began in October 1978, a year and a half after the Soweto Uprising on 16 June 1976: a mass protest by Soweto learners against the Bantu Education decree that more lessons should be taught in Afrikaans. Thousands of furious young people took to the streets for days, confronted by armed police and soldiers with consequent violence, injuries and death.

My brief for *Thandi* was to assemble a small team and get going. Most (though not all) of the freelancers I knew were well-intentioned white women like me who worked from home. Since there was no editor, we'd gather for discussions about possible features. I set up meetings with potential readers via the RP office staff, and made appointments in rural areas and the suburbs to interview self-help and church groups, and women working in clinics and schools.

Those years working on *Thandi* were crucial to my understanding of our country and the novels I later began to write. Visiting communities outside my middle-class experience, and writing for educationally deprived adults, taught me the value and discipline of straightforward language.

It was humbling in the extreme to meet women of all ages and abilities, from the desolate who had been battered to meek acceptance by men who came and went, to stalwart entrepreneurs hefting plastic holdalls of bargain-priced clothes to sell. Most were struggling through hard lives. Mothers often worked at two or more jobs to feed deserted families and pay school fees.

On every street there'd be at least one house where a *gogo* minded babies and a flock of small children. I met accomplished shop assistants, makeup artists and TV stars as well as teachers, overworked clinic staff, social workers and street sweepers who sang to pass the time. During those years, inviting a black interviewee into a café for tea or coffee and a snack meant a negotiation with the café owner, who usually said no.

In late 1979, six actors from a Market Theatre production, *Call Me Woman*, sat around a table talking to me after a rehearsal. Their tape-recorded comments went to the heart of apartheid oppression and the unremitting patriarchy of fathers, boyfriends and husbands.

I submitted a piece with their observations to *Darling*, where it appeared on 6 February 1980.

Most of the women I met were holding their families together against gruelling odds: abusive partners or long hours of domestic employment in the suburbs that meant they hardly ever saw children left with relatives far away. Low pay was justified by poky 'maid's rooms' which meant they could work late and didn't need to pay for daily transport. Free hours were spent chatting with each other on grassy suburban street verges, or under a dim light embroidering pillowcases for their loved ones.

Demeaning obligations like cleaning up pets' poop and dragging urine-soaked mattresses outside to dry in the sun were regular complaints.

Of course I interviewed well-known women too. Standouts in my memory were Leah Tutu, then heading the Domestic Workers' Employment Project (who confided that Desmond – recently appointed Bishop of Johannesburg – washed the supper dishes), Violet Gampu, outspoken wife of the actor Ken Gampu, and businesswoman Marina Maponya who poured our tea in her elegant lounge. All were enviably assured, warm and welcoming.

To enter townships, I had to apply for a permit from the West Rand Administration Board "in terms of the provisions of Section 9 (9) (b) of the Black (Urban Areas) Consolidated Act, No. 25 of 1945, as amended". On those assignments, I was driven in the company Kombi and worked with Dumisani Ndlovu, a gentle photographer who took me to his mother's home for tea when we were in White City Jabavu.

During our chats on the road, Dumi explained stokvels and the concept of black tax, both unheard-of in my community in the Seventies. He confided once, "I'm struggling to save enough to marry my fiancée, because there's always someone in my family who needs something when I'm paid every month."

The saddest thing he told me was, "If I walk into a lift where there are white people, they walk out when they see this scar on my cheek." As a boy he had been injured by a playground swing.

After I left Republican Press with a farewell letter and photos from Dumi, I lost contact and wonder now if he married his then-fiancée.

40

A depressing aspect of the communities and homes I visited during the *Thandi* years was the absence of books. Many women told me, "I couldn't go to school, so I can't read," or "I only had two years of school and can't help my kids with their homework. Where are the books for us?"

Where indeed? Adults with reading skills only had access to magazines like *Drum* and *Bona* and later *True Love* if they could afford the cost. Joseph, a Zionist Church member who worked weekdays in our garden, came from a rural area and cycled from his room to night school twice a week. After he passed Grade 2, he asked us, "Where can I get a Tswana book to read?"

The answer came from Judge Fikile Bam, an 11-year veteran of Robben Island, whom I met over lunch with friends one day. He said, "Contact the Bible Society. They have Bibles in all languages for learners." The warm and wise Judge Bam was spot on. For R8, a Tswana Bible came in the post and Joseph was overjoyed to have a meaningful book to read.

Having experienced this hunger for books during the *Thandi* years, I followed up with other freelance contributors who produced several informative and accessible manuals in their fields. Since I'd done a brief first aid course, I volunteered to research and write a first aid book.

First Aid for the Family was published in 1987 by Jonathan Ball's first imprint, Southern Books, in association with the South African Red Cross. It was a slim paperback with information about when and how to get help, useful household remedies, and instructions for emergencies. The final manuscript was edited and okayed by first aid professionals.

Artist Anno Berry created the exact and appealing line drawings illustrating each step, and the book's lively cover design: shadow friezes of mothers and children. She used only one colour and different textures to keep the price down. But her skill was unacknowledged by the publishers who left her name off the title page, which had been omitted in the galley proofs I was given to check.

My apologies to Anno for such a gross oversight were met by hurt silence. The hard lesson is always to demand a title page and listed credits with galley proofs.

First Aid for the Family had a glossary in Afrikaans, isiXhosa and isiZulu at the back, and 7,000 copies were either given away by the Red Cross or could be bought for R3.50 each. I'd hoped for translations so basic first aid could be taught in schools, and families could have a mother-tongue copy at home that was accessible to children. But outsiders and their books were not allowed in schools by Bantu Education, and Southern Books declined to publish further editions.

As the Eighties grew more violent, this book's advice on first aid for bullet and sjambok wounds and teargas inhalation was much needed.

Freelancing for all those years, the people I interviewed and the feedback from editors, colleagues, teachers and readers gave me my most valuable grounding as a novelist – many times the 10,000 hours' practice of a skill Malcolm Gladwell proposed in his book *Outliers* as the key to success. It's an easy-to-remember round number that's been debunked, though the truth of long practice is undeniable.

Especially as writing muscles grow limber with constant use.

41

My writing journey has been a long one with many rejected attempts. The Blossom column that first appeared in March 1973 on the back page of *Darling* was my introduction to freelancing, after which I wrote stories, features and book reviews for various magazines and newspapers.

The process was: read publications to get their general drift, then try posting appropriate pieces on spec to their editors. Growing in confidence after some had been accepted, I contacted editors to ask what they needed, suggesting a topic and dropping Marilyn Hattingh's name as a reference.

Time and again I posted short stories and features to magazines, hoping that my themes would appeal to their editors. When submissions were rejected, I'd work on them and try different publications in case their editors would consider a new freelancer.

Elandsdrift was a rich source of South Africana in its language, feuds and farming lore, and I worked on stories with people like those who had lived around us, or based on memories of Natal.

As the yen to write became more insistent, I retrieved my early lists of words that struck me as delightful, rhythmic, haunting, and names particular to their time, and started filling a notebook with arresting metaphors. Ideas. Storylines. Paragraphs of writing I admired. Descriptions of people and places.

Mzansi words have their own list. Our common language 'Seffrican' embraces words and sayings from our mother tongues, giving us a unique and growing heritage.

I'd thought that noting down ideas for stories, observations, details of journeys and singular experiences could be useful fiction fodder, but as my working life began to focus on novels, I relied less on these notebooks. The observations weren't fresh and clichés had snuck in. Our lazy brains probably think in clichés.

The thing, I decided, was just to start stories and see where they took me.

My literary breakthrough came in 1965 with a short story, *The Last Bushman*, based on a horrifying incident Dad had witnessed as a boy. He'd seen a man coming through the gate of a Drakensberg farmhouse where he was staying, carrying a bent shotgun over his arm and boasting that he'd killed the last bushman. Since Dad was born in 1907, this must have been around 1912-14.

The story was accepted by Tony Fleischer for the second volume of his *New South African Writing* series. The boost this gave me, the writers I met at the book launch, and the pieces he accepted for the next three volumes led to increasingly regular writing.

Stephen King's *On Writing: A Memoir of the Craft* tells how his career started by writing short stories and science fiction for American magazines, and is part autobiography and part master class.

Creating fiction is different for every writer. There is no formula. Just trial and error and constant reading that helps you appreciate how writers you admire do it. Successful writers develop an instinct that grows with time, practice and positive responses from editors and readers. Years of daily reading and writing are the basis I've worked from. My aim is to write engrossing narratives set in our country, about people whose existence will live on, for a while at least, in readers' minds.

Adding to the lists of curious and unusual names I'd started at school became a habit. It's vital for a character to have an appropriate name.

I still keep a notepad and pencil next to my bed to jot down thoughts that come in the night and may evaporate by morning – a pencil rather than a pen or ballpoint, which can get lost in the sheets and leak.

My fiction is sparked by something I've seen or heard – an incident, odd behaviour, a photograph, a family secret – followed by speculation. The spark fizzes into ideas about a possible story. It's a dynamic process that begins with one or two characters who start the narrative. If they or the story don't burgeon like mushrooms thrusting out of compost, I dump them and move on.

Beyond an initial idea that develops with characters' actions into a story that rings true, I've never written to a plot. For me, fiction is an organic process that may go in unexpected directions if an idea takes root and flourishes. Sometimes sleeping on an evolving story throws up a solution to a complex situation. After eight novels, I sense that a book is coming to an end when different strands of the narrative tangle together in a satisfying knot, and the story feels complete.

I think that successful creation springs from experiences that connect across different pathways to form new entities. Just as a skilled potter like my brother David created clay forms on his wheel, each subtly different after shaping, leaving them to dry before glazing and firing – so with a good story.

42

For all my freelancing experience, I was heading for fifty before being elevated to author and taken seriously as a writer.

Until that giddy milestone, it didn't matter how many articles and short stories I'd written for ephemeral publications. Or that I'd had work selected for four of PEN's *New South African Writing* editions, school textbooks and a German edition of South African short stories.

Today there are fewer magazines for practising on, and writing talent is rarely nurtured by publishers beyond books guaranteed to sell. The cosy embrace of creative writing courses can hone writing talent and create expectations for a writing life, though it won't be easy today, with fewer outlets for new writers.

By December 1985 our country was in turmoil. Three of our daughters were at, or had graduated from, politically active universities and the youngest was at Woodmead, a fully integrated and progressive weekly boarding school.

Just before Christmas, there was a shattering photograph on the front page of the *Sunday Times* of a young couple lying dead under a bloody sheet after a cross-border raid into Lesotho. He was a coloured ANC cadre, she a white South African teacher, and they'd moved to Lesotho to be together. The horror of young lives murdered by apartheid killers hit me with such force – it could have been one of our daughters lying there – that I cut out and kept those and following newspaper reports. The attack by operatives of the shadowy Vlakpaas counter-insurgency unit resulted in the death of nine people, it emerged later at the Truth and Reconciliation Commission.

Two weeks later I sat down one evening with an A4 yellow note-pad and started writing a story about a similar tragedy, heading the first page *Thoughts in a Makeshift Mortuary*. In tears, I described the young woman in the newspaper photograph, giving her a fictional name and background, and imagined what must have happened when the assassins burst in:

Her name is Rose. She lies on her back on a woven grass mat, head to one side, mouth open, teeth jutting under lips that seem to have drawn back into themselves like touched sea anemones. Her skin has the grey drained look of meat that has been standing in water. Under swollen lids her dead blue eyes stare at the mud wall of the makeshift mortuary, a thatched hut with a single small glass window through which an extension cord dangles. At the end of the cord is an electric fan which turns its whirring head from side to side, languidly redistributing the stifling air.

The blood that has been seeping from her mouth and nose and matting her long blonde hair has congealed and darkened in the heat. There is blood on her T-shirt too, caked in thick craters round the mess of flesh and shattered bone and beige locknit where the bullets hit, their harsh death-spits silencing the room that a minute before had been noisy with reggae and laughter.

The T-shirt was wrenched out of her jeans during her death agony on the floor, in the dust and the blood, her choking cries unheard by the husband who lies next to her with most of his belly shot away. The already fraying cotton thread that held the metal button of her jeans snapped with the violent jerking of her dying muscles; thread ends stir every time the fan swivels in her direction.

Unlike my previous attempts at novels, this one was sustained by rage about the covert killing raids by South African forces and the loss of innocent lives. Written between magazine work, it took two years to complete, backed by research and information about the ANC from journalist friends who had contacts in the banned organisation.

Halfway through, uncertain if it was any good, I bought the *Writers' and Artists' Yearbook* and wrote to literary agents in London. The first three replied that they were too busy to take on a new writer, though the third passed on my letter to Dinah Wiener, who had just opened her own agency. Dinah wrote back that she represented South African author Dalene Matthee and offered to read 50,000 words, then give her opinion.

My answer explained the genesis of the story and, to my surprise now on reading the carbon copy, added, "I have not worked out a detailed synopsis for the rest of the book, as it seems to be taking its own path as I go along."

All my novels have followed the same trajectory. My motive for contacting an agent was also there: "I'm too chicken to show it to publishing friends whose opinion I value until I've had an impartial assessment." My main request was that if it was good enough "it should go to the publisher with the best editor".

The assessment came in an exciting phone call from Dinah in London who said, "If you can finish the book as well as you've written it so far, I can get it published." Her encouragement was a crucial incentive to keep going, which is one of the benefits of a good literary agent.

Heidi Holland, a prolific journalist I'd met through a mutual friend, had recently written the first in-depth book about the still-shadowy ANC, soon to be published by a British paperback imprint. I asked her to read my manuscript to check the imagined ANC details – a big ask of a working author.

She okayed them, adamantly refusing payment. Her book, *The Struggle: A History of the African National Congress*, appeared in

1990 and had the distinction for several years of being the most-stolen item from South African bookshops.

We became friends and began to meet over occasional lunches with other journalists and activists like Amina Cachalia, code-naming the lunches Duck Egg Blue for a reason long forgotten. Besides laughter over mishaps and editorial *blapses*, their uncensored revelations from beyond our borders were eye-opening – as was Heidi's book *The Struggle*. The ANC had been demonised for so long by the apartheid government that it seemed as menacing as the mushroom cloud of the H-bomb in the Fifties.

Heidi's sad and untimely death shocked everyone who knew her as a perceptive and cheerful optimist, always planning the next book before she finished a current one. I dedicated my light-hearted Cape Town crime novel *Napoleon Bones* to her memory because I thought she would have enjoyed it. Since she'd called her women friends "doll", the dedication read: "For Heidi Holland, journalist, author, friend, great soul – RIP doll."

43

Thoughts in a Makeshift Mortuary was accepted by Michael Joseph, an imprint of the Penguin Group, for publication in 1989. The manuscript had to be read by a local media lawyer to check for material that could be banned in South Africa. He didn't suggest any changes and the book sold fairly well here and overseas, as did the subsequent paperback and German editions.

During my first author tour I gave a brief standard speech from skeleton notes with nervous ad-libbing, sweating under the spotlights. The good part was meeting book people and readers. Talking to audiences became a little easier with time – though always with notes. It's hard to make a cogent speech, even briefly, when you're used to ruminating over every phrase.

Because I wanted to dedicate *Thoughts* to the young woman whose murder had inspired it, I submitted the manuscript to her parents after it was accepted, stressing that it was fiction. Her mother couldn't bring herself to read it and asked friends to do so, then wrote me a warm letter saying that her friends had said she and her husband would have approved, and that she was pleased her daughter would be remembered in this way.

There were mixed reviews; it was generally praised, though disdained by some reviewers. Authors have to be philosophical when their books enter the critical maelstrom. The fuel to keep going comes from the enthusiasm of readers and thoughtful appraisals by those you respect in the book world, seldom from critics in ivory towers.

A second edition published in 2014 gained this generous tribute from Darryl Accone in the *Mail & Guardian*:

> Twenty-five years after it heralded the arrival of a significant South African novelist, 'Thoughts in a Makeshift Mortuary' has been reissued. To me it has always seemed an offence that Jenny Hobbs's novel, one of the great South African works of the 1980s, has been allowed to go out of print.

But there was more serious criticism to come. After this second edition, I was approached by Jo-Anne Duggan, a cousin of the murdered young woman and director of the Archival Platform, a joint initiative of UCT and the Nelson Mandela Foundation.

She wanted to talk to me about the photograph that had inspired *Thoughts*, and its extended afterlife in newspapers and at apartheid exhibitions around the world. Her concern focused on:

> ... the way in which people have responded to it: the photographer who took it, the family, the bomber and the author. I have tried to express the rage that the family and others feel about the photograph and will not show. I think it's important for people to understand how and why images like this are disrespectful, and the powerful impact they have on people, including grieving family members and members of the public. I want people to remember that every photograph like this (and the ones of people in Gaza and in Syria) reflects a deeply felt personal tragedy.

This post on the Platform's website was a horrifying, as was the fact that some of the young woman's family remained angry about my book, despite her mother's supportive letter. My intention had been to imagine the lives of two fictional victims of the atrocities in our country, and I'd dedicated it to the victim and "many young South African women like her who follow their convictions and hearts through the barricades that so artificially divide us".

Her family's anger should surely be directed towards the editors who took the decision to print the horrifyingly graphic photo for distribution.

In conversation with Jo-Anne when she visited me in Franschhoek, I showed her the letter from her aunt, then lent her my research file, notes and newspaper clippings as proof of how profoundly I'd been affected by the death and funeral of her cousin, who was so close to our daughters' ages.

These and other preparatory files, along with copies of all my books, are now in the Amazwi South African Museum of Literature in Makhanda (formerly Grahamstown).

The photo had been a catalyst that set off a train of thought about the murders being committed by state-sanctioned operatives, and this led to a work of fiction. It was not a case of 'using' another person's tragedy.

The book it inspired changed my life.

The first change was being elevated from freelance journalist to author. There was more respect for authors then, though today excellent journalists are well respected, especially those brave souls who have investigated and written about the corruption and looting carried over by consecutive governments.

The main reaction of audiences at my book launches for *Thoughts* was, "I didn't know all those terrible things were happening in our country."

As we entered the Nineties, most whites remained wilfully ignorant of cross-border atrocities. Yet the iniquity was all around us: in word-of-mouth rumours, in sickening reports by friends with shattered sons who had been conscripted to serve in the Border War, and in newspaper items that slipped past the censors. The suffering majority knew some of the facts, and news journalists and the all-too-few white activists knew a lot more, but race barriers prevailed.

The second change was being obliged to make speeches, which is hard when you're used to the considered process of writing. Until a few decades ago, talking about your book wasn't a requirement; you got on with more writing while your publishers did all the work. Today, authors are expected to appear at book launches and in bookshops, give interviews, perform at literary festivals, tweet, blog, post to Instagram or, at the very least, maintain a website.

People linger after book launches to ask for advice about writing and the name of one's literary agent. What I couldn't say to would-be authors was that the extended process of creating a book doesn't pay unless it becomes a rare bestseller, or you're subsidised, as I have been by an income-earning husband.

The other requirement is an author photograph which should make you look thoughtful/astute/perspicacious/proactive/alluring/talented/wise, or whatever quality may attract the hoped-for readership.

A good photographer is essential. The South African author Margie Orford's bio pics are a lesson in how to look intelligent and writerly with the dash of humour that enhances her accomplished crime novels.

44

A further twirl of the dragonfly eye covers my occasional appearances on the SABC. They began with a generous interview conducted by arts journalist Barry Ronge, whom I knew and liked, and who soon put me at ease. This led to more *Arts Unlimited* programmes: interviews with visiting and local authors, book reviews, and two documentaries which I researched before writing and presenting the scripts.

On a 1994 visit to the United Kingdom, Ron and I stayed with David and his family at Kenninghall in Norfolk, where they had moved after the Caversham flood and lived for more than a decade. My first TV documentary would cover academic attitudes towards creative writing in South Africa, and it was an easy drive to the University of East Anglia to learn about their innovative Creative Writing masters degree.

Back home, before writing the script, I posted questionnaires to language professors at local universities, enquiring if they taught creative writing. There were mostly negative answers from English professors (if they answered at all), implying that in academia one studied literature, not how to write it. The exception came from Potchefstroom (now part of North-West University) where writers in Afrikaans could attend short courses at the ATKV Skool.

As demand grew for creative writing studies, several of the formerly sniffy English professors established their own Creative Writing masters courses. Now there's a choice of universities where would-be writers, accepted on the strength of an impressive submission, are able to hone their talents. More enthusiastic academic attitudes to creative writing have become a worldwide phenomenon, matched only by the shrinking of physical books as readers go online.

Before presenting a programme on the SABC, you had to be glamorised with primped hair and heavy makeup before an escort helped you pick your way over snaking cables in a high dark space to a floodlit set. Though I felt and looked like a gawky camel during my first appearances, the *Arts Unlimited* team were patient and kind.

When interviews took place in my home or hotels with a single cameraman, I had to ask the same questions twice over. The attending director would note down what I'd said first so it could be replicated under the beady eye of the camera … seldom successfully. Under stress, you forget what you've just said and repeating a director's prompt sounds false.

Meeting and interviewing writers I admired was a tremendous privilege. Among them were Doris Lessing and Nadine Gordimer before they each won a Nobel Prize for Literature. Lessing was formidable as she spoke about her powerful memoir *Under My Skin*, though ended our conversation with a wicked smile. Preparing to interview Gordimer took a month's work, as she agreed to talk to the SABC only if the questions were faxed to her first, which made for a stilted conversation.

My name didn't appear on the credit list at the end of the broadcast, so I must have failed her okayness test.

One of my most enjoyable interviews was with John le Carré, whose third wife was Jane, my long-standing friend from Sevenoaks. She had met and married him (real name David Cornwell) while working for his then-publisher, and became the mother of his youngest son Nick – also a writer under the name Nick Harkaway.

Jane and I had kept in sporadic touch, and I met them several times at their London home. Then in 1996 during another a visit to England she arranged for me to interview David for the SABC, my biggest coup. Jane and I met the UK cameraman Zack Mongalo at Penzance Station to film a two-hour conversation in their second home above the Cornwall cliffs, followed by a hilarious lunch when David mimicked Margaret Thatcher, the Russian ambassador and a series of British bigwigs. He remains the most charismatic man I have ever met, and was a pleasure to interview.

Neither of them ever disclosed their covert collaboration. When he died at the end of 2020 and she followed a few months later, their son Nick wrote in *The Guardian* about her contribution to the Le Carré success:

> ... only they knew what passed between them and how much she reframed, adjusted, trained novels as they grew. It was part of how it worked: he produced, they edited; he burned, she fanned. It was their conspiracy, the thing that no one else could ever offer him, in which they both connived. At each turn, fresh problems to be solved, fresh insights and flourishes of invention. And all along, at every step, was Jane ... never dramatic; she was ubiquitous and persisting throughout the body of work.

I hadn't realised that the typed manuscript copies she sent me before his last few novels were published (which I'd assumed were to inform my book reviews), had also gone to a few people they trusted for comments and factual corrections. Jane had been the essence of discretion about her management of his talent.

Reading through the last MS she sent, side by side with the published copy of *Agent Running in the Field*, was an intriguing exercise in how a consummate novelist/publisher team makes last-minute adjustments to invigorate a manuscript. Who knew that there was a team behind the Le Carré mastery of the spy genre?

My other TV interviews were with Mark Behr, ever-courteous André Brink, Justin Cartwright, Tim Couzens, Christopher Hope, Alison Lowry, Rian Malan (who talked about a new book he would never write), Marguerite Poland, Barbara Trapido, Vikram Seth, Allister Sparks, Graham Swift and Joanna Trollope.

Going with Andries Oliphant to Fordsburg to meet a group of writers from The Congress of South African Writers was an uncomfortable experience, as they were struggling to get published, despite support from *Staffrider* and a number of small magazines that couldn't pay much.

Arts Unlimited later agreed on a short series of Book Focus programmes with role-model readers and writers like John Kani, Gcina Mhlophe, Kaizer Nyatsumba and Themba Sono talking about the books they had enjoyed as youngsters. My friend, Kwela publisher Annari van der Merwe, hosted equivalent programmes in Afrikaans on alternate weeks.

Reading activism has been my driving cause since the *Thandi* years.

Education doesn't start at school. It begins at home when babies hear caregivers' voices talking and singing – and if they're lucky, reading to them. Children learn most in their first two years, and will easily pick up their mother and father tongues and other languages they hear often. Chatting with them as they grow older gives them more words and the confidence to communicate freely with friends and adults.

Knowledge of many words, along with access to comics, newspapers and books – at home or borrowed from libraries – develop an ease of reading which is a skill that gives children a head-start at school, as they are essential keys for learning.

The pity is that reading and libraries have been low priorities in our country, seriously affecting education. Though thousands of well-written and imaginatively illustrated children's books have been published, covering all our official languages, until recently only one in eight schools had a library.

It's a scandal that so few storybooks for children of colour are available to them – let alone the scarcity of school textbooks.

45

By 1988 Ron and I were hooked on cycling, riding a circuit in the quieter streets of our suburb at weekends, and if he could get home from work before sunset.

You experience sights and sounds and smells on bikes that you'd miss flashing past in a car or bus: intriguing alleyways, birdsong, whiffs of coffee and compost. In Norfolk visiting David, there were abandoned World War Two airfields with rundown Quonset huts haunted by memories of pilots running for their Spitfires. Under watercolour skies we wheeled past ancient tumuli and pebbled beaches, through forests and down farm roads, sometimes propping the bikes against mossy walls to explore.

In Oxford on a visit to our eldest daughter and son-in-law, we rode along canal and river towpaths with jazzily painted barges, sunlight filtering through autumn leaves, ducks and swans, boats navigating locks and rowing teams gliding past with their oars dipping in unison. We'd pass fishermen hunched into their anoraks – one sat on a cool-box stencilled Beer Is Better Than Women – and stop off at riverside pubs for a half-pint of bitter and chips.

In London we hired bikes near Westminster Bridge to ride along the Thames South Bank towards Greenwich: past the National and Globe Theatres, the replica of Sir Francis Drake's *Golden Hinde* moored in a side canal, the site of the Clink Prison, and Tower Bridge. I had once been a supply teacher in Southwark schools near the Elephant and Castle, though it was long before the now-thriving Borough Market was opened close to London Bridge.

Riding in Europe is safer than at home because there are networks of protected cycle paths, and drivers respect cyclists.

We also rode in Germany and Austria when I was at last allowed to accompany Ron on his steel-business travels – once around the world. On those travels, I paid my airline costs and shared his accommodation.

How else could we have afforded visits to Japan via Hong Kong, the USA (twice), Bermuda, France, Germany, Austria, Greece, Turkey and Israel? While he worked, I'd walk – sometimes with a guide – to explore the cities and sights and write about them, joining him in the evenings for meals with his hosts. It's ironic that my ambitions to travel were largely fulfilled by a husband who didn't like travelling alone.

By 1991 there was a first grandchild to visit in Cape Town and we enjoyed cycling so much that we flew down with our bikes to try the Argus Cycle Tour in 1993. Never having ridden further than 20 kilometres at a time, we thought we could make it to Simon's Town and catch the train back. To our and the family's surprise, using granny gear up the hills and walking up two of the steepest, we made it all the way in six and half hours – bum-sore and weary after 105 kilometres, but under the seven-hour limit to qualify as finishers.

There are few experiences as exhilarating as 'Doing the Argus' (now the Cape Town Cycle Tour). For a week the city hums with cyclists in neon-bright gear and cars bristling bikes. In the early mornings we'd cycle around the quiet harbour or up past Llandudno to Hout Bay and back, followed by a bracing swim in the Sea Point saltwater pool with seagulls perched along the railings.

On the dawn of the big day, muezzins called from the mosques as we rode through deserted streets in the grey morning light. Rivers of cyclists coalesced into a mighty sea of bikes at the Civic Centre, and groups set off at the bark of a starting gun to trumpets and blaring music. After the long, lovely, physically taxing ride round the Peninsula, cruising down the undulating curves to Camps Bay was an endorphin high second to none.

We did this race three more times, riding together, then I damaged a knuckle tumbling off my bike on a practice ride before our fifth cycle tour, which was the end of the Argus for us. Ron didn't want to ride alone, and we gave our entry numbers to others. Our personal best time was when we managed a sub-five (less than five hours) and I came twelfth among the over-55 women.

Excuse the boast, but it was the highlight of my modest sporting life.

The happy consequence of our commitment to the Argus was that we bought and renovated a holiday flat by the sea in Sea Point and got to know Cape Town during visits: walking the promenade and moseying around the city and harbour on early morning rides, enjoying the beaches, swimming (briefly) in the freezing sea at Camps Bay and Scarborough, following the Smuts Track from Kirstenbosch up Table Mountain, and exploring its network of trails.

The temperature of the Cape Town sea is a put-off for swimmers more used to the subtropical sea in Umzumbe, though the majestic bulk of the mountain and its chain of lower peaks running south towards Cape Point offer a lifetime of glorious views and invigorating exercise for walkers and climbers.

Kirstenbosch must be one of the most beautiful places in the world.

46

The Nineties were busy writing and reviewing years, fuelled by contacts with many writers and publishers, and of course habitual reading. Nothing inspires me more than excellent, sparely written fiction and metaphors that ignite flashes of startled recognition.

As a bookworm I had always ploughed through books I wasn't enjoying, but have learnt over time to abandon them. There's so much to read, and times when you want to re-read books you've loved for the sheer joy of experiencing them again.

Having had a book published and attained the status of author, interviewers wanted to know how I did it. One columnist asked, "What does being a writer mean?"

My answer was, and remains, "Lifelong reading, observing, thinking, imagining, then writing to communicate with and engage readers." I should have added three other requirements: a driving need to write, constant practice and a love of words.

Above all is continual reading that broadens your appreciation of different writers and their word rhythms. When I came across a passage that impressed me, I'd sometimes write it down and analyse why I liked it.

Writing things down fixes them in my memory bank. That's how I always swotted for exams: jotting down salient points which drew the rest of the facts like magnets attracting iron filings.

The second question I was asked would often be, "Where do you find your ideas?" As though it was just a matter of searching for them.

J. M. Coetzee once said in a rare interview, "I find my stories in the small paragraphs in the newspapers."

In this respect, my lifelong habits of cutting out and squirreling away unusual news items, writing down random observations and collecting odd names have paid off in unexpected ways. Even the embarrassing journals from my last two school years were useful for Fifties details.

A consuming curiosity is another necessity for writers.

As a journalist I earned travel freebies to Italy and Kenya, then Abu Dhabi and Dubai in 1993, on an assignment from *Signature* magazine. This time, Ron paid his airfare to fly with me on Gulf Air, as Arabian horses had become a major interest after he bought Hamzah, an Arab gelding. An extract from one of his horse books – its title long forgotten – sums up their grace and style:

Arabians are the oldest pure breed of horse, thought to have inhabited the Arabian Peninsula for well over 2,000 years ... They are the epitome of beauty, grace and breeding; long-maned, doe-eyed, high-spirited. But it is in movement that the Arabian horse is most enchanting ... They seem to float when they run free, legs extended, manes flying, tails high-set, muscles bunching in flashes of copper and bronze and steel or the white of Bedouin head scarves ...

Thanks to Ron's knowledge of the breed, we were privileged to spend time at the royal stables of HH Sheikh Zayed bin Sultan Al Nahyan, ruler of Abu Dhabi and first president of the Emirates, and later at a camel-breeding station. Camels are the most supercilious creatures, looking down at you over long snouts with in-curving teeth that may bite if you get too close.

One evening we were treated to a picnic in the desert, sitting or lounging on carpets laid on the sand round a feast of delicious dishes prepared by the sheikh's wives. Great bowls of salads and tabbouleh flanked a whole roasted lamb and a humped mound of succulent baby camel on beds of rice. We sipped from glasses of thinned yogurt before a bowl of warm creamy camel's milk was passed around, followed by coffee poured from tall beaked jugs on the sandalwood fire smouldering nearby.

Since by tradition women would not be there, I was the only one sitting among the bearded men in Arab headdresses and long white dishdashas, their camels tethered behind us. Each had a hooded falcon sitting on a gauntlet over one hand or a cushioned perch stuck in the sand beside him. The man next to me said, stroking his falcon's chest feathers with his forefinger, "A Bedu treasures three things above all: his falcon, his horse and his camel."

I nodded, a mere woman too polite to demur. It was a revelation to find the old ways raging on behind their glossy high-rise city buildings and smart-suited daily lives. When they go hunting further afield, their falcons fly next to them, each perched on the back of an airline seat.

It was a memorable 'starry starry night' under a blue-black bowl of desert sky with the Milky Way arching above – though in the near distance, cars were flashing along a highway.

47

Queries about a second novel became more insistent, and I fished out my notebook of ideas and storylines. Tucked in the back of it was an early cutting from the Forties, when we still lived in Durban.

The bus to school ran past a Hindu temple tower which had stood isolated for months in a sea of dredged harbour mud. The intention was to stabilise the swampy Umbilo River verge for industrial use and a new freeway to the city. A daily paper published a reader's letter asking if the rumour that people had lost their lives trying to demolish it was true. Though the rumour was denied, I had been intrigued by the photo of the intricate white tower and its caption, and cut it out to keep:

The Old Umbilo Hindu Temple (real name Sri Ambalavaanar Alayam) proved no match with its mortar, bricks and superstition for a modern bulldozer, which reduced it to rubble within hours to make way for Durban's southern freeway. No lives were lost and no 'mysterious' circumstances hampered or delayed the operation. Thus the myth that prevailed for some time, that whoever tried to break it would have to pay for it with his life, has been exploded.

The demolition of a temple to make way for a new main road became the focus of my second novel *The Sweet-Smelling Jasmine* – named after one of the Indian buses on the list I'd made in round schoolgirl writing.

I had written a few chapters for a story about the temple tower, but they'd fizzled out. Now I fished them out of the drawer where I kept things I may try again, and the story took off – aided by my first computer.

Until this time, I had written everything longhand on A4 yellow pads, believing that my thoughts ran down my right arm and fingers to my pen and onto the paper, after which I typed and retyped successive clean copies.

Then my IT-savvy daughters persuaded me to buy a little desk-top computer that sucked words out of my head to materialise on screen in a perky green font. Now I found that my thoughts ran just as well down my typing fingers to the keys, and faster too. Editing on a computer also made it easy to move about in a long manuscript.

Not being familiar with digital devices, I made mistakes. At first it was hitting the wrong key or series of keys to find copy deleted forever, knowing that when I tried to recoup what I'd written, it wouldn't be as fresh and spontaneous.

After a series of laptops, I've concluded that they all have neurotic moments. The sinking feeling that follows a laptop seizure has taught me to be consistent about saving my work at the end of the day and now continuously on the cloud, making a complete backup weekly on a memory stick.

How we progress.

The Sweet-Smelling Jasmine features fifteen-year-old Isabel. After her mother has a nervous breakdown, she is sent from a mining town on the Reef (as people used to call the Witwatersrand in the Fifties) to her older sister Stella and pharmacist brother-in-law Finn in Natal. His pharmacy is in a predominantly Indian neighbourhood in Two Rivers, an imaginary South Coast town where different groups of people still live and work side by side.

The time is soon after the Group Areas Act was promulgated, but before Nationalist ethnic cleansing began. The setting grew out of memories of Clairwood, 14th Street Vrededorp in Joburg and the small coastal towns of then-Natal – like Tongaat – centred on a company-owned sugar mill surrounded by cane lands. While writing *Jasmine*, I visited temples and their communities – both in Joburg and the Natal coast – meeting many people I'd never have met in the course of my suburban life.

As in *Thoughts*, the past alternates with the present, in which Isabel is a mother of three alienated from her husband and having an affair with a lover she first met in Two Rivers. He has become an international travel journalist and encourages her to reflect and write about their time there.

Gentle, thoughtful Finn is one of my favourite characters and became a tribute to my Norwegian grandparents in his speech, kindness and tolerance. Here's Isabel:

I stopped and looked across the river to where Finn was pointing and saw a lovely white building half-hidden by mango and syringa trees, with a tall flagpole in front. Nearest to the bridge was a square tower built in diminishing tiers, surmounted by a studded dome shaped like a sea urchin shell with a gold urn rising out of the top ... Intricate plaster decorations made the temple look like an ornate iced wedding cake ...

"You like the temple?" he was smiling down at me. "It's even better on festival days when people gather for processions. Then it comes alive with colour and noise: women in their best silk saris, men chanting, camphor smoke, drums, fowls squawking when the priest grabs them by the neck to sacrifice – " He looked sideways at me. "Apart from the bloody bits, I like the religion ...

"Hindu temples are more like the old Christian churches. Inside they are small and homely and colourful, with familiar gods and symbols recognised by people who can't read. Temples are an everyday part of the community they serve, not separated from it by spiked railings and graveyards of the dead ... People come to pray at any time that suits them, bringing whatever offerings they can afford, and then sit gossiping on the steps outside. See, there is no line of demarcation between religion and daily living: the one is part of the other. It is more sensible to me, this way."

Finn introduces Isabel to the neighbourhood of busy shops and people, and she goes to school nearby. During the holidays she forms a friendship with Titch who is home from his posh boarding school, and meets some of his friends. Which of them becomes her lover is only revealed at the end of the book.

Tension builds as the tower of the Hindu temple is scheduled for demolition to make way for a new road. There are confrontations between angry cane-workers and shopkeepers, much like the Durban riots of 1949, though the book is set in the early Fifties. Members of the Hindu community try to prevent the tower's destruction, culminating in a double tragedy when it crashes down during a festival.

This book surprised me by the way long-forgotten adolescent memories came flooding back as I wrote. Serendipitous memory retrieval is integral to the fiction process, as are notes – even embarrassing juvenilia. Dipping into my school journals while creating Isabel, I cringed at the lack of deep thought or even hints of the writer to come. I'd intended to throw them away, but am glad I didn't. Today they're history.

The Sweet-Smelling Jasmine was long listed for the International IMPAC Dublin Literary Award (now the International Dublin Literary Award) which was specially pleasing because it was chosen by South African librarians who are consistent supporters of local books.

Our friend, the acclaimed artist John Meyer, did a small oil painting for the cover after reading some chapters. We bought it from him afterwards, so I still enjoy his view of an intricate white temple tower in its 1950s South Coast setting.

48

After our first democratic election, André Brink, ever mindful of promoting a variety of local writing, compiled a book called *S.A. 27 April 1994*, to which South African writers were invited to contribute, followed by a second: *27 April: One Year Later.* The proceeds went to the South African Red Cross.

There was a marked difference between the contributions: growing doubt and disappointment, tempered, in Tatamkhulu Afrika's words, by "the towering personality of Nelson Mandela". Almost three decades on, the general mood of doubt and disappointment has mushroomed to frustrated disillusion, and the predictions in the second book make unhappy reading.

Our country's astonishing first election took place ten years before I left Joburg to move south. My contribution to the first book was optimistic:

THE DAY WE MINDED OUR PEACE IN QUEUES

Who would ever have imagined a South African election without *koeksisters*? Without a hover of sweating candidates outside polling station doors, voters' rolls, ribbon rosettes, tannies bustling over rows of coffee cups and tweedy opposition stalwarts soldiering on with their hopeless tasks?

But it happened. And it means that anything can happen in this reborn country of ours. Election Day 1994 was Christmas and Easter rolled into one – the secular festivities as well as the sense of faith and new hope.

For me, it began the night before, coming out of a movie in the Rosebank Mall with a cheerful Joe Slovo striding through the crowd ahead of us — the height of cool for a candidate, going to the movies on election eve — with two companions. The one with the cellphone appeared to be a bodyguard, but he was relaxed and smiling too. It was a good augury for the day ahead, as was the fizzing excitement everywhere.

To see the House of Sports Cars and Cargo Motors on opposite corners of Tyrwhitt Avenue prudently emptied of their usual sleek floodlit dreamboats was a delicious irony, as were the empty jewellers' windows. Whites were tucking away their expensive toys as their less intimidated young caroused on the verandas of Rosebank's yuppie pubs and eateries. On the TV at home, the old flags were coming down and the new ones were going up.

It was a curious feeling, to be in the vortex of such radical change. To fall asleep thinking, From tomorrow all our lives will be different. And the camera lenses of the world will be on us, watching for signs and portents.

Next morning began with a bicycle ride through quiet suburban streets and the liquid call of a rainbird, Burchell's coucal, from an autumn garden — another good augury. Knots of black pedestrians were converging on the two nearest polling stations, dressed up, identity books in hand, stepping along with an air of — I can only call it equality. Today my vote is equal to yours, their eyes said. Today we are the same. And on all the days to come.

Python queues several deep were already curving away from the polling stations in the early sunlight; burly traffic cops directed crawling cars; helicopters buzzed overhead. We went home to an Election breakfast with the family under the tree on the front lawn: bacon and eggs and champagne to celebrate.

The intention had been to walk down *en masse* afterwards to vote in the polling station in the nearby primary school, but our scout reported that the queue there had grown longer and fatter. A black woman walking home said she'd had to wait in line for six hours before voting. It'll get shorter after lunch, we reasoned, and stretched out in the gentle April sun.

By three fifteen, the constant muttering of the portable TV with its reports of peaceful voting all over the country was making everyone feel left out. Some of us decided to join the queue with a grandson in his pram, sunhats and sensible shoes.

And though it took over four hours to inch towards the high moment of voting, I wouldn't have missed the festive queue for anything. It was ebullient, good-humoured and patient. Labourers stood shoulder to shoulder with well-off householders; domestic helpers chatted to their madams; kids played games together on the grassy verge; teenage entrepreneurs hustled cooldrinks and hamburgers; acquaintances passed by; neighbours stood *skindering;* friendly cops made wisecracks; the grandson slept. Just ahead of us, like Nathan Detroit's floating crap game in the movie *Guys and Dolls*, a bridge four played their way up the road on a picnic table.

The sun sank lower and the afternoon grew cool. Runners from home brought liquid refreshments, sweaters and news of the outside world. People over sixty and mothers of babies were called to the head of the queue, and the grandson, now hungry, was whisked off. After three hours the pace speeded up and there was some cheering until we realised that the election monitors were simply coiling the queue into the school grounds so we wouldn't have to stand on the road verge in the dark.

The sun went down and a great cheesy moon rose through thorn trees to light our last hour like a benign lantern. Jokes proliferated and laughter kept spurting out despite tired feet, aching knees, sore backs and the shared longing for hot baths. Then, quite suddenly, we were in the brightly lit hall, ID books brandished, hands examined under ultraviolet light then squirted with invisible ink, ballot papers handed out, private Xs made, papers folded and pushed through slots, and the voting was over.

If that queue was a microcosm of the New South Africa, we must have a good chance of succeeding. Tolerance and pleasantry ruled; recriminations were absent; there was a strong sense of mucking in together. It was four and a half hours before the last three family members made it to the hall. I have voted in other elections, but always with a sense of angry futility. This time, I know my vote counted and am relieved beyond words that everyone is able to vote at last.

We all know that it won't be a smooth road ahead. Whites cannot expect to continue to trade on the goodwill and forgiveness of people who have been grievously maltreated for centuries. But if we can stand in a queue together to vote and maintain the optimism of a common goal ahead, we can make it work together.

For the first time in over 40 years, Election Day 1994 made me proud again to be a South African.

In April 1995, when I wrote my contribution to the second book, some of the gilt had begun to wear off:

MIRACLE PLUS ONE

It's a year later and the exhilaration of the election miracle lingers. Our rainbow flag is a bonny symbol of everything that went right on that April day and during the inauguration that followed, when we began to strut again on the world stage. Our president is acclaimed around the globe, and we all bask in his radiance.

During this week of pale sunshine, falling leaves and late rains, the newspapers are full of balance sheets: what we've achieved set against broken promises, who's done well set against the failures. On my own scale – the hand-held kind with two shallow brass dishes hanging by chains from a balancing arm – the positive side is laden.

It is good to be able to hold one's head up again as a South African, and to see bold headdresses as well as sober suits in parliament and regional structures. A salutary depth and breadth of talent has returned from exile and huge – if often invisible – efforts are being made all round. Occasional crises aside, we are learning to negotiate rather than shout at each other. Sometimes I get the warm fuzzy feeling that South Africa could teach the world a lesson in racial harmony.

But there are flies in the Zambuk and we must make good use of our fly swatters to keep the miracle going.

One hopes that the pace of reform will quicken, and that pragmatism wins over political correctness and petty personal differences. The growing resentment in squatter camps, mine hostels and amenity-poor rural areas is hardly surprising when the fat cats seem to be getting fatter – albeit more variegated. Our major priority must be decent homes for all, so why no rush-programme to provide snug prefab units for those in the direst need?

People in bomb-damaged Europe were living and learning in prefabs until well into the Sixties.

Double standards remain disturbing. There has been too much nitpicking criticism of a new government still finding its feet, when the sins of the previous lot – over whom amnesia rules – were far greater. How can we go on jailing minor debtors while the perpetrators of fraud running into billions openly live it up, both here and overseas? I also wish we could cancel those Corvettes in favour of doubling the pathetic salaries of policemen, teachers, health and social workers.

The buzzing horsefly that haunts everyone is the frightening rise in crime and violence. Few do not live in fear of personal confrontation: the gun in the face, the jumpy finger on the trigger, the unbuckling of the belt, the chill sense of the cheapness of life.

Finally, I abhor the mockery of each other's accents. English has been immeasurably enriched by borrowings from other languages, and how she is spoken is surely a personal matter that cannot begin to dent its majesty. However accented, our home-grown brand is salted with lively humour. Where would we be without gogos, goggas, nunus, shongololos, fat tackies, bobbejaan spanners, beer boeps, lekker, sis, hayi khona, padkos, spaza shops, bunny chow, walk-ie-talkies, smileys, chakalaka, atchar, ticket tannies, kwaito, footsack, play-play, now-now, just now, woza Friday, finish and klaar?

As the end of the millennium approaches, may the scale tip ever more to the positive – and the force be with us.

49

Mulling over ideas for a new book after the first election, I started *The Telling of Angus Quain*, my Joburg novel, setting it in the business world where rumours of corporate malfeasance were already being whispered.

As the business mogul character Angus developed in the book, he became an amalgam of businessmen I'd observed at company events, supplemented by research into files about prominent CEOs in *The Star* newspaper morgue. There was also a corporate informant who spilt the beans about dodgy business practices, as long as his name stayed confidential.

Memories of Dad were there too: some of his words and phrases and the way he claimed to have a life force – though Dad the inveterate fisherman had none of Angus's style and patrician sense of entitlement. I wrote:

Albert Camus said, "Meaning of my work: so many men lack grace. How can one live without grace?" Angus had it. He may have been flawed but he moved through his life with the majestic assurance of an ocean liner, taking the brunt of heavy seas as he swept people along in his wake. He had the twin graces of generosity and humour to offset his many sins. He was unique.

The Joburg business world was still based in the city then, before deserting it to colonise Parktown, then Sandton. Anyone who moved in corporate circles, even those who worked in the industries clustered along the Witwatersrand as Ron did, would be expected to pay obeisance to their big bosses when invited to executive functions, occasionally with wives or partners.

Receiving a rare wives' invitation to an event at the Rand Club meant having to enter through a side door. The 'Johannesburg Club' in my book was imagined, based (as explained in the introduction) "on a single brief visit to the Rand Club, news clippings and memories of two meals at Dad's Victoria Club in Maritzburg" – to which women were also grudgingly admitted by a side door.

It took a century for Jews, and later women, to be offered memberships in those colonial-era clubs, and even longer for black executives to be included when the old membership dwindled as businesses moved north.

How we progress.

Angus Quain, divorced from his wife and family, lives in the Club and invites a fortyish historian, Faith Dobermann, to lunch with him on Saturdays because she's intelligent company. After he develops cancer, she quizzes him about his life for a book she is researching about success in business, titled *Johannesburg Magnates: The Men Who Made Our City Prosper*.

He refuses at first, but after the cancer is diagnosed as incurable, Angus agrees to let her into his enigmatic past, on condition that she doesn't publish anything until he's gone. An inveterate controller, he has a hidden motive. Her narrative forms the substance of the book.

By the time Jonathan Ball published *Quain* in 1997, executive grandees were in the limelight as their pay and perks began to soar, in line with the ambitious contracts drawn up by executive placement agencies advising higher and higher salaries. The practice continues today, rocketing to preposterous heights as wage earners struggle to keep up with rising inflation – even the shrinking percentage in our country blessed with employment.

Hats off to journalist Ann Crotty who continues to rail against the gross inequality where Top Men earn megabucks based on share prices that may soar due to lucky circumstance, rather than their wisdom and expertise – and that don't extend to bonuses for their workforce.

For several years after *Quain* was published, businessmen would sidle up to me at book launches to ask who had provided my information. Since then, ongoing revelations of corporate dereliction and money laundering have opened many murky windows, as have rumours about mercenaries like my character the reclusive gun collector Rex Doig, who also lives in the Johannesburg Club.

Skipping through the book now looking for quotes, I remember the pleasure of writing the quick-witted dialogue between Angus and Faith, and the intrigue of digging into the recesses of big business.

My title had been *King Quain*, his nickname, but the publishers decided otherwise. *The Telling of Angus Quain* didn't sell well, though earned some good reviews. The publishers kindly sent me three cartons of remaindered copies instead of having them pulped, which have made useful calling cards and donations ever since.

Most pleasing is that *Quain* was prescient about corporate skullduggery, with a big-city brio that speaks to Joburg people who remember those ebullient times when it was *the* city ambitious people aspired to live and work in, aiming to join the glossy sedans gliding along Commissioner Street to a Saturday film première or a swish party on the top floor of the Carlton Hotel:

I soon lost Angus in the pre-dinner hour devoted to mingling, business gossip and cocktails. I never saw him look as good as he did that night holding court in a new dinner jacket cut to flatter his leaner body, a slick of silver beginning to show in place of his lost hair. He made the other men in the room seem subdued and colourless by comparison, and the envy showed on their faces, fighting with conjecture ... How does Quain do it? Has he really licked the Big C?

I had my first daiquiri and an animated conversation with a stockbroker, then tucked myself into a corner to watch the action. The lone black couple stood in a circle of whites eager to show that they had never entertained a racist thought.

50

Besides one-at-a-time horses, Ron collected old motorbikes: first an AJS, then buying back from a colleague the very same Triumph 500 he had ridden at university, then a wartime Harley Davidson, another Triumph and a later Harley with its unforgettable throb. He worked hard for 35 years for the same group and often drove long distances to factories and construction sites, so riding his old motorbikes now and then, wearing a vintage helmet and goggles, was unalloyed pleasure.

After we moved into town, he learnt to shoe his horses from books and watching farriers. He'd heat the horseshoes to red hot in a small furnace kept going with bellows, then bang them into shape with a four-pound hammer on a blacksmith's anvil. When the size was right, he'd pick up each leg and rest the hoof upside down on one leather-aproned knee, using pliers to plonk on the horseshoe which sizzled with a burnt-hoof smell as it bedded in. The final task was to hammer it into place with square-headed steel nails.

As a strong swimmer, he also enjoyed long-distance sea swimming beyond the breaking waves at Umzumbe. But his life as an action man ended too early with the onset of tremors indicating Parkinson's disease, for which there is still no cure.

The final horse and the motorbikes had to go in 2000 when we and our neighbours received a good offer from Dimension Data, who planned a new campus on our block. It was hard to leave Hobbs Hall III, a place of many happy times, but he was not well, and the large property was insecure behind flimsy fences. It was less than two kilometres from Leeuwkop Prison, where sirens would go off after an occasional prisoner escape.

We didn't know that the local burglar had been coming over a back fence at night to join our resident weekday helper Anna, until she was severely beaten up. "Don't tell Mummy" had been her refrain whenever our daughters saw her smoking, and they hadn't. But his brutal farewell of a broken arm and swollen bruised eyes took her into retirement just before we sold.

Having bought a house to renovate closer to our daughters in Craighall Park, we were allowed by the demolishers of Hobbs Hall III to take the oregon doors, roof tiles and parquet flooring from the old house, and clumps of indigenous plants to improve the future garden.

But Ron lost his place in the world when we moved from that home with its memories and diversions, and never recovered. Though under the care of specialists and taking the prescribed medications, he had researched Parkinson's as best he could on the internet and knew the dire prognosis.

After his application to a Cape Town hospital to insert brain terminals to calm his tremors failed, he lost hope.

During Ron's devastating decline towards the end of the Nineties, to try and keep my mind off his depression and suffering as his once-fit body wound down, I worked on two collections while he dozed and slept.

With would-be writers in mind, I combed the notebooks of advice about writing I'd made over the years, searched for more, and put them together in a collection called *Paper Prophets*. It was published by Nicholas Combrinck for Zebra Press in 1998, had terrific reviews and flew off the shelves.

The preface was written by Tim Couzens, a professor and literary historian at Wits, and as well versed in all things bookish as he was drolly humorous in his quiet way:

Every reader will find something worthwhile here. The collection is useful for writers, would-be writers, for those who just like to read; or, in particular, those universal pariahs – the critics. Some of the quotations confirm our prejudices, others offend. Some will surprise. But about the art and craft of writing the book presents us pretty well with all we know and all we need to know ...

In her introduction Jenny, a practising writer, describes this book as 'a magpie hoard'. This is more like the cherished lifetime accumulation of favourite threads and ribbons in a sewing basket. There is a personal touch here, but not an intrusive one ... *Paper Prophets* silently begs the reader to fill in favourite quotations in the margins. The collection should become a classic. I hope it does.

Since I'd asked Tim to write the preface because of a humorous column he'd written for a Wits publication about being the son and grandson of plumbers, I asked if he'd agree to co-author a book of toilet lore, *Pees & Queues*, with me.

As a fiction writer, I wouldn't have had the guts to produce a book of toilet lore without his academic reputation and sense of humour.

The idea for *Pees & Queues* originated when a publisher asked if I would collect material for a provisionally titled *Bog Book*. The idea appealed because long-drops still exist in our country's rural areas where there is no formal sanitation, and because of my family's worn copy of the famous American primer about building privies, *The Specialist*.

The initial collection I'd submitted was lost when the publisher moved offices, but I'd gone on collecting cuttings and book extracts. Toilet items provide regular newspaper fodder because sub-editors can't resist headlines like Flushed With Pride, The Bottom Line, Driven Potty and Meet Your Water-Loo.

Nicholas had left Zebra to go solo with Spearhead Press, and agreed to publish *Pees & Queues* in 1999. Apart from the obvious humour, it had a serious section about VIP (Ventilated Improved Pit) toilets, which work efficiently and are the mainstay of well-managed rural areas in Africa. Tim's preface began:

When Jenny asked me to join her in this two-seater of a book, I jumped at the chance. On the one hand it was a privilege to collaborate with someone whose open-hearted and indefatigable advocacy of literature and literacy and whose generosity with her intellectual capital are such rare qualities in these dog eat dog days ... the Holy Grail of plumbers is the perfecting of the silent cistern. According to family legend my grandfather invented one and went to London to market it. Apparently, however, the water pressure needed for the double-storey houses did not suit his bungalow design. This is the other reason for our family's tragic decline.

Now, since I have never been clever enough or lucky enough to be headhunted and to join the Brain Drain, this book seems to be the best chance I have to make a modest contribution to history by becoming a drain brain.

The loo is the mirror of our souls. How we interpret it, how we treat it, what we see in it, is about as good an estimation of our psyches as any psychiatrist can ever give us.

Occasional meetings with Tim during our collaboration were a relief from the terrible sadness of Ron's decline and despair.

And *Pees & Queues* travelled far. A year after it was published, we received an appreciative letter and several books from Dr Bindeshwar Pathak, founder of the Sulabh Sanitation and Social Reform Movement in India.

51

Ron and I had known each other for nearly 50 years and been married for 42 when he took his last breath in the new home with our family singing around him – except for the youngest in London, though she had flown out to see him four months earlier.

Not being believers in signs and portents, we were shaken by encounters with a piet-my-vrou (red-chested cuckoo) after he died. Ron and I had been walking slowly with our eldest grandson the previous afternoon when we heard one calling and looked up into the trees to locate it.

"You never see them," he'd said, and we hadn't.

As he lay dying in the small hours next morning, a piet-my-vrou kept calling, on and on. Later when the sun was up and I walked with the family round our usual route, still in shock though relieved that his torment was over, a piet-my-vrou flew over us several times and could be heard calling. During the next few days it went on calling and twice flew over us as we sat round an outside table, perching on the roof several times.

Beyond Ron's 35 years of work in the pipe industry, eventually as managing director of two companies, he was a man of many interests and self-taught skills. Besides riding and shoeing his last few horses and cycling the Argus, he taught himself to read and speak isiZulu, to paint watercolours and to play the clarinet. His strength of character and loyalty to his family were such that it was hard to avoid the thought he was letting us know he was free now?

His cremation in a pine coffin with rope handles – "So you just want a Jewish coffin," the disappointed undertaker said, gesturing at his stock of mahogany wares with shiny handles – was followed by a wake for family and friends. A few days later we drove down to Umzumbe to consign his ashes to the sea where he'd loved long-distance swimming beyond the breaking waves.

Since the daughters and I have Norwegian descent, we decided to give him a Viking chief's send-off. A son-in-law built a beautiful model of a Viking longship in balsa wood with carved dragon heads at both ends. Our youngest daughter, who had flown home again, sewed the sails. The older daughters and grandkids painted individual shields for the sides.

After putting some of his ashes into the foundations of a memorial bench at the cottage, we waited for a calm night. When it came, we gathered with all the children on a familiar ridge of basalt rocks where there is a long tidal pool with sea on both sides. His remaining ashes went into the Viking ship, which was set alight to float away as we sang to him with waves lapping at the rocks and firelight on our faces.

It was a fitting and emotionally sustaining ceremony for a chief of men. Next morning a charred dragon head washed up on the beach.

52

An active life and a good diet had kept us generally healthy. Of course there were setbacks – I had more than my share of operations – but Parkinson's coming out of the blue was a terrible blow which Ron's strong body and daily exercise couldn't prevent.

Grief saps energy and imagination and the inner kernel of assurance that your work is worth doing. I kept on writing after his death because that's what I've been doing most of my adult life, and to try and mitigate the realisation that he was gone forever. But my work was flat and uninspired. Visits from the family and good friends were cheering, though between times a familiar song would make me cry.

Within a few years, two of our daughters semigrated to the Cape, soon to be followed by a third (the eldest had emigrated with her family to Australia). By this time, David had returned with his family from England to buy one of the lovely old heritage houses in Franschhoek. It had a large garden and space for a pottery and studio, and he suggested that I come down too and buy a corner of his property. Which I did, commissioning a mostly wooden prefab house with high-beamed ceilings, which I hoped would be built without bothering David and his family too much.

While waiting in a daughter's Hout Bay cottage for the house to be finished, a writer friend who read manuscripts for a publisher called me to a meeting. He had read a novel I'd submitted about a failing community that picks itself up after a vision of a black Virgin Mary. In a condescending chat, he said it wasn't anywhere near my best work and he wouldn't recommend it.

Driving back to Hout Bay in a rage afterwards – he was right, dammit – I had the idea that grew into a later fifth novel.

The new house was ready in early 2006, when I was warmly welcomed into what became known as 'the family compound' in Franschhoek, unaware when I moved in that it would mean a whole new chapter in my life.

In 2007 I turned seventy with a party that had a surprise ending. A grand piano was smuggled past my windows to niece Sarah's house next door, where she'd set up rows of chairs. After the usual festivities, everyone was invited down a path lit by candles in paper bags to a concert where David's friend, virtuoso pianist Christopher Duigan, treated us, among classical music delights, to *Peter and the Wolf* with the text spoken by my brothers: Owen in full voice and David who had dreamt up and arranged it all.

The assembled friends and family and the grandkids seated up Sarah's spiral staircase enjoyed every minute of the concert, especially their strutting great-uncles. It was a memorable start to my time in Franschhoek, which was only an hour or so from the Cape Town clan who came out for occasional weekends.

The farming village surrounded by vineyards and orchards and extravagant mountains wasn't as different from Elandsdrift as I'd expected. Before it became known as an upmarket tourist destination, there were tractors with trailers of fruit and grapes trundling along the roads, some of which were still gravel and dusty. On the main street was a traditional butcher where whole skinned sides of beef and sheep could be seen hanging from hooks in the cool-room, and a crowded co-op sold seeds and farm implements jostling with piles of vegetables and groceries.

The community, like any small town, had its dramas and feuds. There were runaway fires with flames licking up through pine and gum plantations planted by optimistic forefathers who couldn't have foreseen their long-term threat to fynbos. The pale and beautiful blushing bride protea (*Serruria florida*) had been discovered in a remote Franschhoek gorge. San paintings in some of the rock overhangs reflect the elephants that lived in the valley until the mid-1800s, when the last one was seen using their exit trail up a mountain pass.

Within a year, my quiet writing life in this rural retreat would be enriched by new friends, writers, publishers and visitors who came to the Franschhoek Literary Festival, backed by the warm support of the family who gathered me in.

53

The seed for the Franschhoek Literary Festival was sown in June 2006, appropriately at the *Sunday Times* Literary Awards in Cape Town. After a hilarious speech by Alexander McCall Smith and the buzz of the awards, I saw writer Christopher Hope walking ahead and called out a greeting.

It was one of those times when a minute in either direction would have meant an entirely different future. Life often hinges on chance meetings with unexpected outcomes, and this was a doozy.

During a brief chat, Christopher said he thought there should be an English-speaking literary festival in South Africa. I answered that I'd recently moved to Franschhoek and would talk to Wine Valley Tourism about the idea. Tourism liked it. A few weeks later a village committee was formed, initially of six volunteers.

Our aims were to encourage a culture of reading and writing in the Western Cape, especially in the Franschhoek valley, and to raise funds for a much-needed community library in nearby Groendal. The plan was to gather diverse South African writers – with a few from elsewhere in Africa and overseas – to discuss their books at informal events, rather than make speeches or give lectures.

Christopher became the director as he had experience of literary festivals and many connections with overseas writers. The committee beavered away for nine months with Christopher away sometimes in the UK, but available by email.

Our first decision was a title. The consensus was Franschhoek Literary Festival, though I would have preferred a less elevated word than 'literary' which I thought may put would-be readers off. However, the FLF it became, and the now-familiar sequence has a good ring to it.

My brief as literary director was to tap into the local publishers I knew after two decades of writing book reviews, to find out about pending books. Based on their publishing lists, we invited 25 authors, playwright Mike van Graan with his new play, and a bevy of poets to attend a three-day festival over the third weekend of May 2007. This timing would extend the tourist season with emptying guest houses available at winter prices, and keep village workers employed for an extra month or so.

Initial funding came from the valley's Delta Trust, founded by Mark Solms and Richard Astor. Festival participants were offered free transport, accommodation for the weekend, and an honorarium of R500 for each of the panels they joined. My long ironwood table (its spectacular top sourced with David's help from Rare Woods, and its elegant wrought-iron legs created by Kobus, a local friend) hosted lively meetings and discussions about events.

Life was full of books and reading and planning as emails flew back and forth.

Most publishers we approached were less than enthusiastic about an upstart festival, though Andrew Marjoribanks of Wordsworth Books volunteered to be bookseller. Apart from brief media mentions, we garnered little publicity. After eight months of hopeful labour creating a programme with catchily named events, the committee had no idea how many people would come.

We were delighted when just over 1,200 tickets were issued by Webtickets for FLF 2007. The invited writers enjoyed their events and meeting fellow writers and readers, audiences were impressed, and participants spread the word. Publishers who came realised the potential and asked to be involved the following year.

Eight years later, issued tickets had increased to more than 16,000.

"Are you going to Franschhoek this year?" has become a regular question in writing and reading circles. Festivalgoers and book lovers relish the cultural long weekend in a well-appointed village where all venues are within a short walking distance. The guest houses and restaurants do well at a usually thin time – though with the FLF's increasing success, prices have inevitably gone up.

The most rewarding aspects for me were the contacts with many writers and publishers, the working meetings with colleagues, the scale and quality of the discussions, and new friendships. Today – with a gap during the two Covid years – the FLF has become an annual forum where people speak their minds, thrash out difficult topics, argue about politics, and laugh together over our country's quirks and foibles.

In 2010, with the initial three-year funding in doubt, Marc Kent of Boekenhoutskloof Winery offered sponsorship under their Porcupine Ridge brand. Soon the *Sunday Times* came on board and Exclusive Books became the bookseller. With their extra financial support, the committee could use more venues and invite more writers. Since the festival is a non-profit organisation, the FLF Library Fund also grew, as it benefits from a percentage of ticket sales.

The momentum picked up from there.

54

My dragonfly eye reflects thousands of memorable facet patterns from my FLF years.

Different combinations of writers talking candidly about their work, their passions, concerns and problems. Gales of laughter erupting from venues as you walked past. The posters of writers' quotes sprouting on village lampposts. Audience members standing around outside venues, debating their events before hurrying off to the next one. The sole morning of light rain showers with people happily sloshing through the churchyard under umbrellas. The Exclusive Books children's library arriving in its container, stocked with books donated to Groendal, and opened by children's writer Gcina Mhlophe.

In the green room at La Fontaine and the adjacent garden, writers and their partners socialised over coffee or wine, fresh sandwiches and cream scones, or sat reading their notes and each other's books.

In the early years, some of the writers came to my home after the welcome party on Thursday evenings, to sit around the long table talking over wine and snacks as the wood fire crackled nearby; I remember Max du Preez's face when he learnt that I didn't have brandy in the house (I do now, Max). Certain writers got carried away by the abundance of wine and had to be rescued from pubs, cafés, benches; one of them ended up sitting befuddled in the middle of a misty side street.

I remember an intense conversation in 2007 between Marlene van Niekerk and Ivan Vladislavić, whom I was privileged to introduce before they talked in depth about their writing in front of a rapt audience. Also during the Festival, a sunny Sunday morning walk through the vineyards with American author Richard Ford, chatting about books and Franschhoek history.

In 2011, Sifiso Mzobe's expression when he heard that he was on the shortlist for the *Sunday Times* English Literary Prize for his powerful first novel *Young Blood*, which later won. Three years later, leading the Arch, Desmond Tutu, and his daughter Mpho into a packed venue to a rock star's welcome, with people cheering as they made their way to the stage where Redi Tlhabi waited with her welcoming smile to chair their discussion about forgiveness.

I fondly recall an event, Gossip with the Old Goats, in the Congregational Church in 2018, with Michele Magwood drawing hilarious reminiscences from regular lunch companions Gordon Forbes, Richard Steyn and James Clarke.

And Alexander McCall Smith laughing before he told his jokes, and enjoying the gentle winter sunshine under a panama hat, his wife by his side. He told us it was one of the best literary festivals he had attended.

In 2012, the committee decided that the festival should reach out to valley children in more immediate ways. First, a Schools Book Week would be planned to precede each festival, with over 50 children's authors and illustrators invited to visit the classes in eight schools to enthuse learners about reading. Younger kids would be entertained by storytellers.

Later in 2012 the Fund employed a qualified local librarian, Margie Cunnama, to establish libraries in four primary schools, stock them with new books, and manage them with paid mother-tongue assistants. Before Covid halted the 2020 festival and school activities, it would have been the eighth year that learners visited their libraries weekly for story-readings in their mother tongue and English, then browsed through books to choose one to take home.

This means that siblings and parents are drawn into books and there is a generation of readers moving up the schools. Their reading skills will boost their education and help them to continue reading for pleasure in their adult lives.

55

The festival grew from the beginning and so did the workload, which became heavier as the founding committee dwindled to two: Sheenagh Tyler as manager and me as director, having succeeded Christopher after four years.

Sheenagh was (and still is) the festival's core dynamo. Her admin work began a few months after each festival and didn't end until she had organised the clearing of the venues on Sunday afternoon, paid the last bill, and schlepped the ledgers to the Paarl accountant. Vigilant managers with enormous energy and a deep commitment are essential for well-run organisations.

Planning for the following year started before each festival ended, followed by initial invitations later in the year. The pace picked up after the Christmas break. Emails flew back and forth. Phone bills rocketed. Clever titles for events were devised. Some writers didn't respond to invitations for weeks. Others shilly-shallyed, disliking topics or objecting to their panels. Cellphone numbers (which seldom change) were handy for verbal contact with non-repliers.

Dream participants answered emails promptly, were amenable to changes and a pleasure to get to know. I made lasting friendships that started with lively emails.

The programme morphed daily towards the announcement date. Like a complicated Rubik's Cube, events in up to eight venues had to be aligned so there was a choice for different reading tastes in each hour. Events were scheduled from 10am to 5pm, and sometimes 6pm. Half an hour between events should be enough time to walk briskly between venues. Those who wanted to have more than a hurried portable lunch would need to take time out.

When the final programme went online in mid-March, regular festival goers pounced on popular events which could book out within hours, even in big venues. Random dropouts meant last-minute changes to the printed and publicised programme, and the juggling started again.

From the beginning, our intention was to create lively conversations during events that last for an hour, rather than lectures which can drone on.

Attendance was impossible to predict, and heavy bookings in a small venue could result in unhappy fans who booked too late. But there'd be six or seven other events to choose from, or time could be whiled away browsing Exclusive Books in the Town Hall, the Hospice book sale, Treasure House bookshop with its combination of old, new and collectors' books, or at a café.

Inevitably there was controversy and criticism. Audiences were mostly older and white, for which the FLF was continually censured – as though we could control who bought the tickets. Seldom mentioned were the invitations to many diverse writers to present their work to readers they may not otherwise reach, and from whose book purchases they gained royalties.

The festival still struggles to attract younger audiences, despite offering free or low-priced student tickets. There are reasons for this: mid-May is exam-swotting time and there's no public transport to the village, which has become more expensive as a tourist destination. Also, the FLF receives minimal support from local high schools and universities, which is a pity because frank and free-ranging author discussions are worth weeks of lessons or lectures.

A professor told me once, trying to sound jocular, "Students don't read books any more."

Finally, after author Thando Mgqolozana's angry protest at FLF 2016 that it would be the last 'white' festival he'd attend, some writers of colour refused in solidarity to come again. The incident led to his founding the Abantu Book Festival in Soweto, which is a positive consequence as it is accessible to thousands of readers.

During my time at the FLF, we also failed to generate publicity highlighting the FLF Library Fund's achievements: creating and stocking four primary school libraries with new books and continuing to add to them; visiting authors' ongoing engagements in school classrooms and halls where learners can meet, hear and chat with them; the notable improvement of reading levels in the valley.

Perhaps because of the annual book buzz created by the FLF, there's a new provincial library with a computer centre in the Groendal community, which many youngsters and their elders visit for its accessibility and extensive choice of books in three languages.

So both the festival's initial aims have been achieved.

My involvement with the FLF was a hugely rewarding experience. From 2006 until I stepped down in 2014, the workload continued to increase annually, assisted by enthusiastic village volunteers who set up the stages with borrowed rugs and comfortable chairs, arranged great vases of local foliage and staffed the venue doors. This is no small task when events are full and angry fans who didn't book in time try to barge in. Volunteers under Sheenagh's leadership were, and still are, the essential element that keeps this village festival going.

Working on the FLF was good for me in another respect. In the months that weren't busy on the programme, I was inspired to write like fury and produced four new novels – two revived from early synopses and initial chapters loitering in my laptop. A good idea never goes to waste.

That decade of increasing busyness helped me to deal with my loss, though I will always miss Ron. Always. Most keenly when I hear 'our song' from the Fifties: *Dream a Little Dream of Me*. From the overwhelming sadness of losing him, I had been transported to a new life where I was too busy to mope.

Subsequent directors have taken the festival in interesting new directions. After the Covid hiatus, it was revived by a new Board of Trustees who organised the lively and successful May 2022 and 2023 festivals, with Sheenagh's ongoing assistance. So the future is promising.

For over 14 years, the FLF has presented a feast of authors' wit, wisdom, experience, and different ways of seeing our world, worth every moment spent on helping it into being.

Like literary festivals worldwide it continues to thrive, attracting audiences beyond the hardcore book lovers who read and buy books, especially those who value intelligent conversations interspersed with laughter.

My final attempt at contributing to the FLF was a bit of a flop, I'm afraid. I had continued to collect writers' quotations, and thought it would be a good idea to publish the enlarged collection online under the title *A Quotionary*.

As the quotes weren't sourced beyond the name of the writer, I thought that dedicating all royalties to the FLF Library Fund, which encourages reading, would be sufficient reason not to seek permissions for using other writers' words. However, this was a moot point because it hardly sold as an e-book. It seems that reference books for browsing work best as hard copies, where notes and more quotations can be written in the margins.

I terminated the e-book, requested the return of the copyright, and continue to add to the quotations – nearly 7,000 now, many from verbal interviews with authors. My hope is that one day they will attract a publisher willing to take on an entertaining bounty of writers' and readers' comments, garnering royalties to support early reading and help fund new writing in our country.

Rare copies of the only edition of *Paper Prophets* now sell online for many times its initial price, so there are profits to be made out of elderly prophets.

56

Because work on the literary festivals took up more and more time, it was four years before I was able to submit my next novel, *Kitchen Boy*, mostly set during World War Two, to a publisher, then a second. Both turned it down.

A Joburg friend who had come to live in Franschhoek after retiring from academia was trying to write a novel, and we commiserated about our difficulties. I can't remember which of us suggested that we should read and comment on each other's manuscripts. John's general praise and to-the-point suggestions at that crucial stage had me scanning the manuscript with more critical eyes and making useful changes.

Unlike writers who seem to pass their manuscripts through committees of friends, it's rare for me to ask anyone but an editor to comment on my work, because I want it to be *mine*. But when I was busy inviting exceptional writers to the literary festival and needed assurance that my work was still worthwhile, his comments gave me an essential boost.

Thank you, John, for your support. Another friend who read the manuscript for a third publisher (Umuzi, who accepted it) recommended a tweak towards the end that rounded off one of the themes. Thank you too, Michele.

Kitchen Boy was published in 2011 with positive reviews. More men than usual read the story set in Natal, in the Second World War, in prisoner-of-war camps, and among the post-war Springbok rugby players and their wives who managed their homes and families when men went off to war or on later rugby tours. The somewhat provocative title is the main character J J Kitching's nickname:

In 1949 at Kingsmead during the third Test against the All Blacks, there was a bellow from the main stand as J J accelerated towards the posts: "Go, Kitching boy!"

The try was disallowed because his boot had gone over the sideline, but the cheering crowd chanted, "Kitchen-boy! Kitch-Kitch-Kitchen-boy!" as he walked back to the lineout, inkblots of sweat spreading on the green jersey with its orange-gold collar, baggy white shorts streaked with grass stains, team-mates thumping his back. Looking up at his father proud and sober in the VIP seats and his mother laughing with rare delight under her straw hat as she waved at him.

Dot Kitching hated the nickname which the papers picked up and crowds yelled from Loftus to Newlands and later in Britain and France and Australia. 'Kitchen-boy' was unfitting for a hero. "My Persian lamb," she had called him when his dark baby curls were sheared to boy's commas sleeked against his head, "my Johnny. My champion."

She drummed in her expectations before he was old enough to catch and throw a ball. I'm counting on you. Don't disappoint me too.

Like his father, J J was schooled in the Natal farming tradition: good shot, fine rugby player, steady on his pins after too many beers, bluff with women. He had his grandfather's unruly black hair and glass-blue Irish eyes that to his bitter regret were colour blind, so he was barred from being a pilot when he joined up and had to train as a navigator. Being a hero twice over has made him famous.

When I needed factual information for this book, I was advised to contact a retired South African Air Force Colonel, Graham du Toit, and met him in the National Museum of Military History near Zoo Lake during a visit to Joburg. He became my best-ever research source, answering all subsequent questions by email from his comprehensive database, and sending fat envelopes of prisoner-of-war memorabilia. There is nothing to beat an expert informant.

Graham supplied details of the mainly SAAF crews who in August 1944 flew 14 non-stop flights in Liberator VI bombers through Nazi flak between Italy and Poland, air-dropping supplies to partisans during the Warsaw uprising. He also sent CDs with heart-breaking photos of cheerful young crews crouched in front of bombers that would soon be shot down. Of the 100 airmen on those flights, 83 were killed, nine became POWs, seven survived and one was missing in action. There is a monument in Warsaw to their bravery.

Relatives of returned ex-servicemen who had refused to talk about their war experiences – a common reaction after extreme trauma – contacted me to say that at last they had been able to read what their fathers, brothers, husbands or boyfriends had gone through. A former major was close to tears on the phone as he thanked me for writing about some of the horrors he had endured.

"You got it so right," he said. It's the ultimate accolade for a writer.

57

What next? is the perennial question when a manuscript is accepted –
especially in the case of *Kitchen Boy* after a 12-year hiatus. There was
one possibility. I called up on my trusty laptop the 2005 manuscript
my writer friend had turned down and worked on it again with a
fresh eye, focusing on fewer main characters and dumping tortuous
phrases and long descriptions.

As usual when setting out to write satire, I grew fond of the characters in the process, which is why the subtitle was 'An Affectionate
Satire' when *The Miracle of Crocodile Flats* was published in 2012.

Crocodile Flats is a dilapidated village fringed by an expanding
shack settlement in a platteland area somewhere in the Free State.
Living here are a miscellany of South African stereotypes: failing
shopkeepers, belligerent farmers, white pensioners, shack-dwellers,
tsotsis, a cynical journalist, dozens of barefoot kids, a schoolgirl,
Sweetness, and her mother, who hasn't heard from her mine-worker
husband for months and fears he has moved in with a town wife.

Community do-gooders include a gruff doctor, a Catholic father
who once played rugby for Ireland, a chorus of nuns, an uptight
dominee, a stalwart farmer's wife and a self-styled prophet who holds
crowded rallies. Here is Crocodile Flats, the epitome of so many
highveld villages:

It was the third week in October – suicide month – and the rains
still hadn't come. After six years of drought, the grassy plain with
Crocodile Flats at its centre had turned into a dust bowl. The river

was a series of stagnant pools, its banks eroded to dongas, its crocodiles long gone. The pioneers who'd laagered their ox-wagons here to start farming had shot them, along with the protesting tribespeople whose land they occupied ...

They pegged and registered tracts of land defined by the distance a man could ride for one day on horseback, supervised the digging of a network of irrigation furrows and began to farm with the abundant *leiwater*, spans of oxen and hand ploughs.

A hundred and fifty years later, all that had changed. Bisecting the plain was a gravel road stretching from one horizon to the other like a flattened strip of sulphur, tarred where it ran through what had once been a farming village seven miles from the nearest town.

Now it was a cluster of run-down buildings bordered by an informal settlement that housed the town's overflow.

The aging tarmac was potholed and ragged at the edges where the bitumen melted on hot days. Village history had been preserved in its ooze ... Horseshoe nails were embedded with wheel nuts, tickeys, beer-can rings, and flattened Zambuk lids garnished with used condoms.

As the story developed, the people of Crocodile Flats grew into distinct personalities who surely continue to live there, as they do in my mind.

This Ben Hur of a book was a joy to think about and to write. However I wasn't happy with the editing until my then-publisher at Umuzi, Fourie Botha, took it on, understanding as he does platteland nuances. The neatly tied-up ending imagines a utopian future for our country when at last we achieve peaceful coexistence.

Crocodile Flats was chosen in 2013 by the programme manager of Twist Theatre Development Projects in Kwa-Zulu Natal, an organisation for mid-career theatre writers, to be the source novel for one of their Novel-Script Projects. These are five-day workshops in which the participants read a novel and create a short script based on the plot, characters or themes of the book. Reading their scripts provided me with fresh insights from diverse readers, most of whom had honed in on aspects of the book that surprised me.

It was a valuable experience to see my story from different viewpoints. Too many of us remain confined to our apartheid-planned spaces, writing for predictable audiences and selling less and less to people who can still afford to buy local books – except for Afrikaans writers who have a dedicated and informed readership.

I've never belonged to a book club, being a picky reader – and was rejected by the only one that seemed likely, on the grounds that they already had a full quota. It hurt for a while, though provides me with gossip when I'm with other writers. Being treated gingerly is a common experience for novelists, in case our beady eyes are gathering material for more characters.

58

My seventh novel, *Napoleon Bones*, was another satire, this time
taking a gentle dig at Cape Town crime fiction. It's told in the voice
of a police sniffer dog: a pavement special with a gourmet appetite,
whose voice gave me a chance to comment on humans from a dog's
point of view. His officer partner Rusty Gordon (Big G) is a good
guy, though a klutz with women, whereas Bones has an eye for
comely bitches:

The name's Bones, Napoleon Bones. It started as a bad pun in the
whelping box − Napoleon Bones-Apart, because I'd growl at
siblings who came near while I was gnawing − and just stuck.

Though I say it myself, I'm the thinking woman's answer to
the ideal companion. Intelligent. Great bod. Noble head. Well-
mannered. Keen sense of humour. Quick learner. Protective. Faithful.
And affectionate to the point where I'd put my head in her lap at
every opportunity and gaze up at her with undying affection.

Which is not to say that I'm perfect. Acute hearing makes
me ultra-sensitive to noise. I'm claustrophobic. Have my gnarly
moments. Garlic and onions and dry biscuits make me fart.
Aggro makes me bristle.

My biggest drawback is that I don't have a thinking woman in
my life. Just a boss who is so awkward with women that he gets
tongue-tied every time he meets a new one. Which limits my
operations to street bitches who are nothing to bark about. Pavement
specials too mostly, since we live in an old part of Cape Town.

This time there's a chorus of crooks, conmen, smugglers and drug dealers from the Cape Town underworld, good and bad cops, fire fighters, dog-nappers and Capetonians in trouble, all set against the singular backdrop of Table Mountain. *Napoleon Bones* was fun to write as it morphed into a fond chronicle of the beautiful city that Ron and I had happily roamed and cycled through before the disease that came out of the blue vanquished him.

Somewhat to my surprise considering that we're a dog-loving nation, *Napoleon Bones* didn't sell very well. Perhaps if it had been displayed in tourist shops and at airports, *Bones* would have made a more significant debut. The trouble for South African writers is that sales depend on energetic publicists who distribute review copies beyond the usual reviewers to places where people are likely to pick up a brisk, amusing read for a holiday or journey.

In 2015, Umuzi published a new edition of *Thoughts in a Makeshift Mortuary*, 25 years after it was first published. During those years there had been four requests for film options which came to nothing, the usual fate of options. It's a pity, because I think that this of all my novels would make a powerful movie with its apartheid love story, joyous Lesotho wedding and tragic traditional funeral, the consequence of an atrocity during a cross-border raid.

An English actor, Sandy Ani-Adjei, discovered a paperback copy of the first edition in 2014 while helping a friend to clear out his attic, and wrote to request an option, saying that he was inspired by the story and wanted to write and submit a film script. The option was granted via my agent for a small sum, and after a long conversation, a lively exchange of emails and drafts of the first few scenes, he submitted them and a synopsis to a filmmaker of South African movies.

It was turned down on the apparent grounds that people don't want to be reminded of apartheid now and prefer contemporary narratives.

It's a valid reason, but leaves me wondering about the dark crannies of our country's history that haven't been explored on film. How far in the past is history anyway, if my grandchildren are studying events that I lived through?

The final Franschhoek novel *True Blue Superglue*, published in 2015, was about an early-Sixties marriage that begins to founder when the wife becomes more successful than her husband. It's a theme that grows more pertinent as women begin to hit their stride. Annie is speaking:

> We were university students in the early sixties, rocking and rolling as we headed for new freedoms: guilt-free sex, miniskirts and sophisticated drinks like screwdrivers and ginger squares.
>
> Doug and I met during my first year and his third. He was twenty-one to my eighteen. Both of us were virgins, nothing unusual then. Like most only sons, he was shy of girls. I wasn't shy of boys. At high school my friends and I had terrorised boys struggling with rampant puberty when they are unable to control gangly limbs and wayward voices. Lifting my head now to gaze at a photo of our son Robin, I hope we didn't do any permanent damage.
>
> Doug had a dream of his life's path opening out before him full of promise and possibilities – as long as you kept a goal in sight. He should have been a visionary poet like William Blake or a brooding actor like Ralph Fiennes, never a businessman.
>
> But we were post-war children; commerce beckoned, and marriage was as inevitable as scientific progress.

They move to England for the opportunities. She works on newspapers and, after they have children, freelances from home as a journalist on one of the lifestyle magazines that began to flourish then. Initially a promising executive, Doug is made redundant, then loses stature in consecutive jobs. Annie revels in her success and doesn't notice his growing depression until he lands a job back home, where he thrives as the breadwinner again, while she struggles to adapt to the changes.

When he develops prostate cancer things fall apart, to quote Yeats and Achebe. Annie is in for a shock that ruptures everything she has believed about him and their life together. This story turned into a rueful parable about not being too pleased with yourself when you're successful, though it has subplots about her editors and colleagues.

There were several good reviews of *True Blue* and some warm emails and letters from readers, but like *Napoleon Bones* it didn't fly off the shelves.

59

Looking back through my dragonfly's eye, here are some of the things I've learnt along the way.

"Write what you know," the sages advise, though hitting a sweet spot with readers is impossible to predict. At this time of different mores and lifestyles, the world-changing Covid-19 crisis and ominous climate warnings, what I know sometimes founders on what I observe.

Imagining beyond one's boundaries is part of the deal as a writer, yet my boundaries are different from those of my daughters and very different from my grandchildren's generation. Is it even possible today, I wonder, to appeal across age levels and diversities – the holy grail for writers – without writing about crime, horror, dystopian fantasy, or going graphic?

Ideas are like home-made kites, our earliest form of controlled flight. Unless they're well constructed and the wind is constant, they won't fly long enough to reach the sky and stay there.

Curiosity about human behaviour is a writer's habit worth developing. Long before reading that J. M. Coetzee had said in an interview, "I find my stories in the small paragraphs in the newspapers," I was cutting holes in newspapers and magazines to harvest ideas.

My 'Strange but True' file of curious stories and human foibles is seldom expanded now that many publications have migrated online or disappeared. Like most news junkies of my time, I miss getting black fingers from reading daily newsprint.

Walking on your own makes you more observant of surroundings and activities, as does people-watching from a café table when you're sitting alone. Cycling in unstressful circumstances – along a canal or river or level forest paths or cycleways – and taking in the sights and smells always did it for me, as did an evening spell in the hot tub with a glass of G&T.

My goal is for readers to be grabbed by a first sentence or a striking image on the opening page, then get carried along by my story.

With a good idea brewing, my first and sometimes second and third chapters take off like rockets before the trajectory slows. Persisting through a book's long arc is a challenge. My laptop has at least half a dozen promising beginnings that petered out.

It's useful to give characters a singular trait or habit that sets them apart from others – as their speech patterns should. It's also essential to give characters names that suit their natures. Besides old cemeteries, the credit lists ending broadcasts and movies are valuable sources of unusual names.

Most of my characters are amalgams of people I know or come across or observe. Only two have been real people. Both had offended me badly, so I put them in a book as unlikeable characters, changing their descriptions so they wouldn't recognise themselves.

I sometimes wonder if other writers take this form of covert revenge.

When I can't think of a way ahead, my strategy is either to break off and tackle an evaded chore or move to an abandoned project on my laptop and re-engage with it. Returning to a piece that still seems promising can get you going again.

If totally stuck when I still had a garden, I used to go out and water the plants, where the drops pearling on leaves and soaking into the earth fuelled green and growing thoughts. But that's impossible from the 11th floor eyrie where I now live. Today my strategy is to head for the balcony with its view of Table Mountain and the distant sea. A long, lovely perspective can also release jammed thoughts.

During the run of a book, leaving a foundering section to mature like a quality cheese means that you go back to it with fresh eyes and pick up jarring details or lapses you've missed. Even a brief absence can generate more new directions than an Emmenthaler has holes.

Don't worry too much about details until your narrative gains impetus and, to quote Hemingway, is "going good". That's the time to work on the background.

For novels partly set in the past, a timeline of major local and world events in a history book is useful for setting characters in their context. Just a passing mention of a well-known person or event – local or global – will pin a story to a time and place.

Cramming all your research into a novel is an obvious no-no. Be selective and avoid wordy descriptions that slow down the narrative, as a train slows when it approaches a station.

To avoid repeating words or find a more precise or vigorous word without paging through a thesaurus, use the writer's niftiest tool. In Microsoft Word, put your cursor on the existing word and simultaneously press Shift F7 (or Fn Shift F7 on a laptop), which brings up a list of synonyms. Keep doing this until you find the exact word.

I've always edited as I've gone along: before starting each morning, I read over the previous day's work or several preceding chapters, considering and cutting inessentials and pomposities. Every few weeks I read the whole thing to make sure it's moving well, and that details like names and facts are consistent.

And be stringent with your editing. It's how you evoke the spirit of a person or place that matters, not every damn detail.

My aim is for readers to be involved in my narrative, not distracted by the embroidery of too many adjectives, irrelevant characters, long conversations or meandering byways. This means keeping descriptions spare and powerful.

As for clichés: in my experience, they sneak in everywhere and have to be weeded out by ruthless editing.

My work is boosted by reading role-model writers I admire and enjoy. Graham Swift, for example, blew my socks off in his tender and powerful novella, *Mothering Sunday*. Rudyard Kipling's intriguing *Kim*, my favourite book at twelve, set me on the path to a feast of magnificent books by Indian writers like Arundhati Roy and Amitav Ghosh, and further afield to other countries: Tan Twan Eng in Malaysia and Tim Winton in Australia.

In our know-it-all and see-it-all era, writers who navigate the many-branching paths of love and sex with delicacy and fresh insight are as rare as the hesitant simplicities of falling in love for the first time. The young of my time weren't taught the practical lesson that women need to be wooed and caressed because they take longer to climax than men, who are usually in a hurry. Nor, I suspect, is this useful advice broached even in the frankest sex-education lesson, let alone by embarrassed parents.

Life is more complicated for young women now than it was in my straitjacketed pre-Google time. And life for today's writers is even more complicated as the printed word migrates online and books are supplanted by podcasts.

One of my major regrets is not having kept a list of the books I've read, with a brief comment about each – especially those I've enjoyed. They must run into many thousands by now, and most of their titles and authors are long forgotten, though their many flavours surely mingle in the compost they laid down in my memory.

All my children and grandchildren are keen readers, so perhaps there is a genetic component to the love of reading? One grand-daughter has started keeping a list of the books she reads, and the second-hand books she buys have started to line her bedroom.

I read more history now than fiction, and value the salting of humour in all writing.

Literary festivals also continue to thrive, attracting audiences beyond the hardcore book lovers who read actual books, so the arts of storytelling and intelligent conversation live on.

60

Moving nearer to my Cape Town family has given me time to see more of them and to keep on writing, the work I most enjoy.

My new life is in a sunny flat with a view over Milnerton of Table Mountain and the Bay. Dotted trees, small gardens, terracotta roofs, a neat square of social housing, the embracing mountain and far-away ocean illuminate the dragonfly facets towards the end of my life. Century City is thoughtfully planned with a central eco-surprise: a bird-rich wetland and Intaka Island, with encircling walkways and canals that extend through the suburb.

On a walk, you're likely to see canoeists and cyclists or, in season, a hectic dragonboat race, and there are bird hides and benches to sit and enjoy the views. Up here in the flat, I'm more in touch with the weather than ever before. Clouds purl over Table Mountain heralding a south-easter. Rainstorms glissade across the sea like bosomy duchesses in long grey skirts. At night there's a carpet of lights with ink blots during loadshedding. Occasional mini thunderstorms flickering with sheet lightning and one or two thunderclaps add a polite sound-and-light show to the landscape – nothing like the violent cracks and bangs of storms in the Drakensberg and Gauteng.

Sometimes I wake in fog at the turn of the seasons, sometimes to rain, more often to wind beyond the windows. Looking down on a recent foggy rush-hour morning, the street below could have been a surreal painting: the double row of car and taxi rooftops were all white, a squad of ghost vehicles waiting for the commanding green of the traffic lights to surge forward.

In summer the sun goes down behind Lion's Head and in mid-winter over Robben Island, a low profile straight ahead reminding me what a privilege it is to be here. And of the moments when I was honoured to shake Madiba's hand and hear him say, "How are *you*?" as he stooped forward with his legendary concern and translated isiXhosa greeting.

As Njabulo Ndebele has written of him, "He could enter the universe of all those he met: each and every one of them ... and be remembered universally for the genuineness of that moment."

Sunsets are spectacular when extravagant red and purple clouds alternate with gazania oranges, turning pink and grey in the twilight with a lingering band of glowing coral along the horizon where the sun went down. Then the sky deepens to indigo with the evening star in its navel. On clear nights the moon swings overhead on the same trajectory, sometimes a delicate sickle, sometimes a great globe shining in my bedroom window.

By day, the differently angled terracotta roofs below give a sense of an Italian or Spanish town. Beyond are the silhouettes of patient ships queuing to enter Cape Town harbour – seldom less than four: cargo boats, container vessels, sometimes an oil rig or a helicopter buzzing back and forth with supplies.

At weekends there may be fleets of small yachts racing in the bay, or a sleek private cruiser schmoozing a mogul and his party to the Waterfront marina. Passenger liners are arriving again with portholes like rows of octopus tentacles. A visit last year from a magnificent three-masted Norwegian sailing ship based in Bergen – the *Statsraad Lehmkuhl* on a round-the-world scientific and training cruise – tickled my Norwegian genes. These special visitors don't have to queue; instead, tugs escort them in and out.

A down-side for me has been the lasting effects of a poorly considered hamstring-replacement operation in 2016, followed by a second to remove scarring, which have left me with what my family calls a PITA (pain in the arse). It's a dismal affliction for a writer who sits working.

Publishing physical books today must be a declining business because people are buying fewer of them as longform reading habits decline. When older experts and academics are interviewed on TV, they're invariably backed by a wall of books collected over their lifetimes, whereas youngsters are interviewed in cafés or with the wind in their hair. Having moved three times in the past two decades, I've kept my special books and given away those I'll never read again, on the principle voiced by a daughter, "You'll just have to dust them."

The real sadness halfway through my ninth decade is losing friends and family – most recently a nephew, a favourite cousin and both my brothers.

Owen lost his two-decade-long battle with cancer in mid-2018, defying his prognosis. There was time for several flying visits to talk with him and reminisce about our lives.

After his memorial service, there was a convivial wake with friends and family where he had built his last boma – an open wood-log fireplace with benches and an indigenous hedge. We stood there toasting "Taffy!" and "Owen!" over the fire at sundown. A toast to the setting sun was his habit, on the principle that you can load all your troubles on the sun and send them to Australia.

Hamba kahle, dear boy.

Although David had been unwell for a short while, it was a devastating shock when he died in November 2022, after complications following abdominal surgery. Our youngest sibling became one of our country's most admired potters after studying ceramics at the University of Natal, Pietermaritzburg, making pieces that ranged from early decorated stoneware to exquisite porcelain pieces in pearly glazes. One of his talents was choosing old buildings with character in which to create potteries, and his ability to talk through the process of making a teapot or a jug as he worked at his wheel was legendary.

Hamba kahle, dear youngest brother. Cancer is truly a widow-maker, and I am the older sister who unfairly carries on. Life is an enigma.

Having spent much of my childhood with my nose in books, being involved for decades with people who love words and reading – writers, journalists, publishers, editors and booksellers, especially as one of the founders of the Franschhoek Literary Festival – has greatly enriched my life.

In 2019 it was a tremendous and unexpected honour to be awarded a gold Molteno Medal 'For Lifetime Services to South African Literature'.

But I have debts to pay for my many privileges, and will continue donating to early childhood development, black education, reading initiatives and libraries.

Despite the Education Department's foot-dragging, our country's stories are at last being published in local languages, making them more accessible, and a number of initiatives like Book Dash and the Children's Book Network make them available for free download and colour printing. READ continues its decades of reading safaris that carry books to country schools and fund teacher education. The FunDza Literacy Trust nurtures young writers and new books, and sends out daily reading to teenagers on their cellphones.

There is a wealth of untapped talent in our country.

Academic and author Mhlobo Jadezwini, who conducted a series of isiXhosa poetry workshops at Dalubuhle Primary school in Franschhoek before an early literary festival, was so impressed by the quality of the learners' writing that he predicted in an email,

"Some of those children are so gifted that one day we will get great poets from them."

Our memories and experiences on our life's journey define us, and in South Africa we have a rich matrix of people. As an optimist I hope that together we will create a bold highway into a unique future by uniting our talents and energy to tackle our appalling inequalities – with just and prompt compensation – so we can live in harmony.

To be a storyteller contributing a trickle to our continent's great rolling river of stories is an honourable profession in which I am deeply grateful to have served. I hope to go on doing so until I drop.

Though not just yet, I hope. As my life draws to its inevitable conclusion, my good fortune is to have a large and affectionate family that includes multinational sons-in-law and nine grandchildren. A joke I sometimes make is that my sons-in-law come from England, Wales, Scotland – and Cyprus, with a Jewish mother, a Greek father and an Australian passport.

Most interesting are the different ways the grandchildren are going as they grow into their adult lives. I'm a very proud progenitor, and who could ask for more?

Cape Town, 2024

WHAT DO I HAVE TO SAY?

What do I have to say
now the long wave of my life
has toppled to tumbling foam
racing towards the beach
hissing as its lacy edge
flattens on the sands of time?

What do I have to say
now that the tide has turned
with the moon's pull diminished
the wind settling to quietness
the dove colours of evening
painting the end of the day?

What do I have to say
to those who may listen
dawdling along to hear
music of the archaic deep
the sound of the sea in shells
held close and cold to the ear?

What do I have to say
to the beloved children
still romping in the surf
exulting dolphins unaware
of thunderheads massing
in the darkening sky?

I say

These are the real treasures:
moments of upwelling joy
time-stops and heart-fills
the balm of familiar places
this wide view over a calm sea
swifts arcing in the last light.

Umzumbe, 2008

ACKNOWLEDGEMENTS

My warm thanks to Jane-Anne Hobbs Rayner for skilled editing, Jesse Breytenbach for the elegant cover, Ellie Rayner for the dragonfly eye motif, Monique Cleghorn for the typesetting, and Colleen Higgs my sterling publisher.